To Ger,
Maybe we've missed
it ... Lets focus on
the good, the great, and
the amazing.
Love you, W

Benrik
Limited

This Couple's Book belongs to:

Her... *Wray B.*

Him... *Jereme Bokitch*

If you find it: Please, please return it to them as they cannot live without it, and indeed feel as if they've lost a major limb. Thank you, kind stranger. Huge reward.

Call... *403 215-8458*

Love is in the air

Happy together

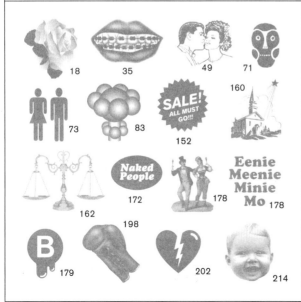

Pillow talk

Things I know about you

Commitment

Trouble in paradise

Ever after

How to use this book

Unspoken grievances can sink a relationship, leaving both partners literally drowning in a sea of frustration. The Couple's Book is especially designed to help you communicate better with each other, thus leading to a nirvana of romantic bliss.

Turn to the middle, where you will find the Logbook. This is the core of the Couple's Book. Here you should write down any comments and issues for the other to read and respond to. Tell him if his unwashed feet are driving you out the door. Tell her if you feel jealous of her rich handsome male boss. Or simply remind each other why you're together.

The other chapters help you document the relationship, from the birth of your feelings to your sunset years together. Record your first date. Plan how to meet the parents. Doodle together on our specially designed Doodle Together page. Make sure none of your time as a couple fades away into obscurity.

You should leave the Couple's Book lying around the house and refer to it daily. If you live separately, each of you should be responsible for it one week at a time. Even in times of crisis in the relationship, both of you are entitled to access it 24 hours a day; in fact, that's when it's at its most useful. Good luck, and good loving!

Who are Benrik? Benrik are Ben Carey and Henrik Delehag. They are a couple, but in a purely professional capacity. Their real-life partners are Kathy Peach and Lana Delehag (née Ivanyoukhina), who are both far prettier than they, as you can see. Benrik are known as the authors of cult best-selling series This Diary Will Change Your Life. The Couple's Book will change your life too, but in a cuddlier way. Interesting fact: Ben likes dogs as pets, but Henrik is more of a cat person. Ben's favourite colour is bottle green, whereas Henrik's is black, though he hastens to add that doesn't mean he's manic depressive, not at all. Their combined IQ is a formidable 346. They formed Benrik Limited with the intention of imposing their warped values on others and interfering in people's private lives, sticking their nose in where it was never wanted. Find out more about them if you have to, on www.couplesbook.com.

When to buy this book?
THE RELATIONSHIP SCALE Average timescale
The Couple's Book is suitable for the right end of the scale

The *Relationship Scale!*

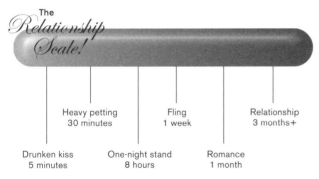

| Drunken kiss 5 minutes | Heavy petting 30 minutes | One-night stand 8 hours | Fling 1 week | Romance 1 month | Relationship 3 months+ |

For our gay friends:
The Couple's Book is entirely suitable for gay couples, provided they are prepared to make a few quick mental adjustments.
1) Obviously, replace HIS and HERS with the relevant gender.
2) Ignore all the gender-specific anatomical illustrations, perhaps tippexing or adding key elements as required.
3) Skip the bits about children, unless prepared to adopt/ artificially inseminate / abduct.
4) The words of wisdom are still relevant! Ignore at your peril.

Couple's Book Maintenance

1) We agree to keep the Couple's Book:
On the coffee table ☐ In the bedroom ☑ In the kitchen ☐
Other:...☐

2) We agree to write in it in:
Black ink ☐ Blue ink ☑ Red ink ☐ Pencil ☐ Our blood ☐
Other:...☐

3) We agree to check it:
Once every hour ☐ Once every day ☐ Once every week ☑
Other:...☐

Warning: should either party lose, damage or destroy the Couple's Book, the relationship will terminate with immediate effect. As your relationship agents, Benrik Limited reserve the right to 10% of any divorce settlements, pro bono payments, child allowances or other legal fees. Where custody is an issue, Benrik Limited are prepared to take the first-born infant in lieu of any payment.

Single? If you have purchased this book by mistake, don't worry. Go to the Benrik Arranged Marriages section at the back of the book where we will arrange a marriage for you with another single reader, so you can both enjoy the Couple's Book to the full!

Benrik Refills If you've filled up all your logbook or any other section marked by this symbol, simply download extra pages free of charge from www.couplesbook.com! Don't mention it.

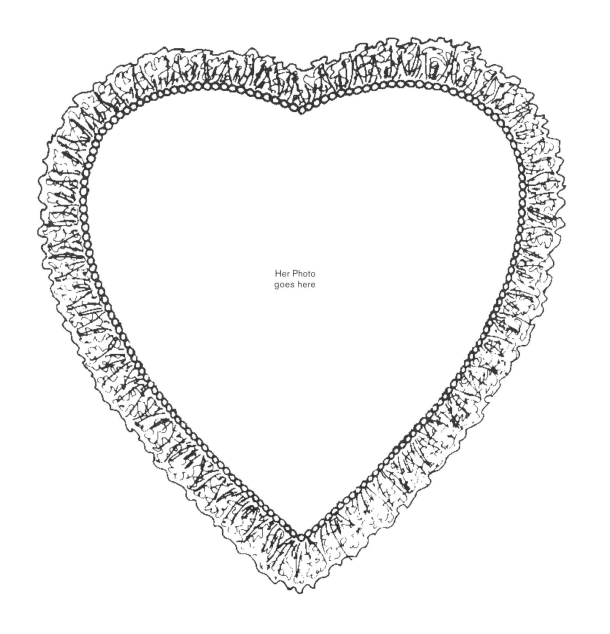

Her Photo
goes here

Surname...... Breadner

First Name(s)..Margareth Wray

Date of Birth.... December 11, 1980

Place of Birth...Mission, B.C

Nationality..German Irish Welsh

Father...Norman Douglas Breadner

Mother...Katherine Ande Melnicke

Star Sign...Sagitarius

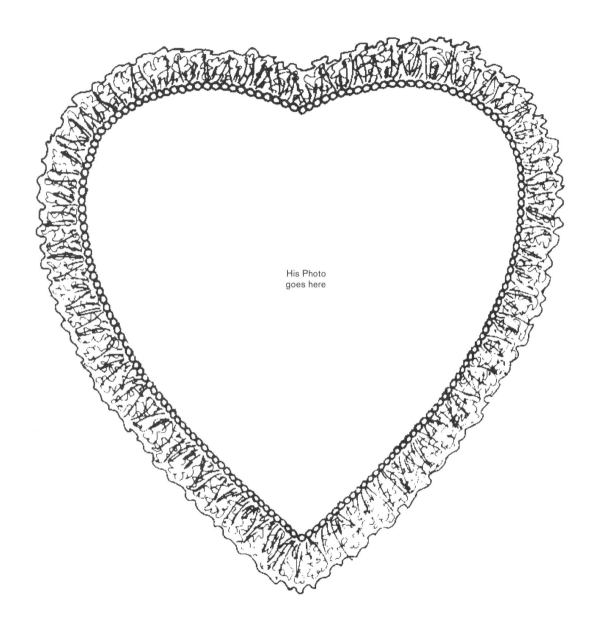

His Photo
goes here

Surname... Bokitch

First Name(s)... Jereme Jon

Date of Birth... August 5 1971

Place of Birth... Regina Sask

Nationality... German/ Ukrainian /Polish

Father... John Andrew Bokitch

Mother... Janet Martha Fiissel

Star Sign... Leo

Love is in the air

During the early stages of courtship, endorphin pleasure hormones are released by the brain at the prospect of imminent coupling. From the first glance to the first mutual orgasm, your relationship is taking shape. Record these precious moments for posterity.

Our first date

Your "first date" will often be referred to in future years as a historical moment, the dawn of an era, on a par with the French Revolution or the birth of Jesus Christ. Enshrine its every single detail here.

Date. _Jan 17_

Place (draw map if necessary). _The apartment_

Agreed time:	Time of her arrival:	Time of his arrival:

Excuse in case of lateness. _Prev Eng Overtime_

Was this excuse accepted?. _Yes_

(Note: the woman is expected to be late, though not by more than 1 hour.)

Stood up? Return this book to the bookshop and next time don't buy one too soon!

How did we meet?

Through friends ☐	Personal ad ☐	Public transport ☐	In crowd ☐
Through work ☐	On holiday ☐	In street ☐	In jail ☐
Through family ☑	Party ☐	In art gallery ☐	In rehab ☐
Blind date ☐	Office party ☐	In supermarket ☐	Affair ☐
Speed date ☐	Christmas party ☐	In toilet ☐	Don't know ☐

Who asked the other out?. _Which time?_

Chat-up line used. _I'm changing my email - I'll forward you_

How long had you fancied them?. _J 3years   W 6years_

How many attempts were needed?. _1_

Who was asked out?.

Were you aware they fancied you?.

Were you flattered?.

Did you reject them initially?.

She wore / He wore (draw)

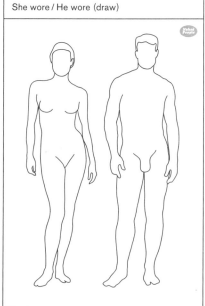

Venue

Cinema..

Movie..

Chosen by...

Restaurant..

Address...

Chosen by...

What you ate/drank..

Who paid...

What we talked about

Topic 1..

Topic 2..

Topic 3..

How far did we go?

Was a move made on the first date?...*Yes*............................

If not, why not?...

How many further dates before first move.............................

First move made at....*2 am*....(time) by...*Jereme*.......

Extent of move

Asked in for coffee ☑	Kiss with tongues ☑	Drunken kiss ☑
Light touch on elbow ☑	Holding of hands ☑	Foreplay ☑
Peck on cheek ☑	Clumsy groping ☑	Full sex ☑
Tender kiss ☑	Declaration of love ☑	Passed out in cab ☑

How the date went	6pm	7	8	9	10	11	00	1am
Love at first sight							x	
Yum!						x		
This is fun					x			
Just friends				x				
Not my type	x		x					
Nothing in common		x						
What a jerk/bitch								x

x = example

Words of wisdom 1

Søren Anderssen explains: "I was a very shy young man. Karen was the prettiest girl in the whole Jalberg. I was 19 and Karen was 22. I was very shy and she was much older! No chance I thought, Klaus Sorensen will get her, he is the boisterous one. Then one day she swam out too far into the fjord. It was the summer but near Jalberg is the water still cold. I was in my boat fishing for Norwegian whelk, sometimes they drift down in the last two weeks of August, when the current is strong. I hauled her up onto the deck. And that was our first date. When we are in the joke mood, we say she was my best catch!"

Do both partners certify that this is a true and faithful account?

Her signature....*Yes* *mostly*................................

His signature....*B* *mostly*.................................

If not, provide separate accounts:

Her version....*Totally Jer's* *fault.*

....

....

....

....

....

....

His version....*THE VIBE was* *POUT BY Wrong.*

....

....

....

....

....

The future: At this point please write your estimates of how long this relationship will last, and place in sealed envelopes. In case of terminal split-up, the envelopes are to be opened and the author of the closest guess will get to keep this book.

Early days

Technically you have taken the first step. Now, will this turn into something concrete, a base on which to build your common future, or will it just be a casual fling? Track the progress of your budding relationship.

N/A

Stage of relationship: Post-first date angst	● ○ ○ ○

Who called who? He called her ☑ She called him ☑ Other (specify:..)

How long was this after the first date?................*1*.........days..........................hours............................minutes...............................seconds

What was the text of the post-first date phone call?...... *Courtesy call*

What was the subtext of the post-first date phone call?...

Did either of you have second thoughts? Yes ☐ No ☑ What were they?..

Hours spent daydreaming about the first date:....*lots*........Was a second date successfully arranged? Yes ☐ No ☐ (repeat until success)

We both confirm that we have successfully completed this stage...Date & Time..........................

N/A

Stage of relationship: Second date	● ● ○ ○

Place..Time..................................Day/Month/Year............./............./..............

How many days after the first date?...Degree of awkwardness.............../10

Description of moves*...

....

We both confirm that we have successfully completed this stage...Date & Time..........................

Stage of relationship: Fling	● ● ● ○

Number of phone calls to each other/day:..........*16*............................(min. 10) Time spent holding hands:....*∅*.....................

Time spent thinking about each other:..*too much*...Each other's face............ Each other's eyes............ Each other's laugh............ Each other's smile...........

Each other's hair................... Each other's ears.................... Each other's hands.................... Each other's feet.................. Each other's smell................

Things that reminded you of them: Car in street Yes ☐ No ☑ Programme on TV Yes ☐ No ☑ Song on radio Yes ☑ No ☐ Sock Yes ☐ No ☑

Passing cloud Yes ☐ No ☑ Tree Yes ☑ No ☑ Sun reflected in puddle Yes ☐ No ☐ Gust of wind Yes ☐ No ☑ News presenter Yes ☐ No ☑

We both confirm that we have successfully completed this stage....*Sep 05*...Date & Time..........................

Stage of relationship: Going public	● ● ● ●

Who did you tell first? (him)....*Jamie*..

Who did you tell first? (her)......*Kyla*...

....

....

We both confirm that we have successfully completed this stage...Date & Time..........................

*If no serious move was made on the first date. If no move was made on the second date, simply repeat this stage until a move is made. Max. 12 dates.

1st
time

You may fill this in the next morning, though it is recommended for accuracy's sake that you make notes as you go along during actual intercourse:

....
....
....

Time: *5am* Place: *Jer's house* Music: *morning*

Overall duration: *3h* Duration of foreplay: *2h40m* Duration of act itself: *20m*

Duration of post-coital cuddle: *5m* Level of drunkenness? Her: *0*/10 Him: *10*/10

Did drunkenness affect performance? Yes ☑ No ☐ Can't remember ☐

Fancy positions attempted: *All*

Unusual features of partner's body: *Wray nore grad dress*

Number of orgasms (her): *0* Number of orgasms (him): *2*

Were either of you virgins? Neither ☑ Both ☐ One (specify:........................) ☐

Overall rating (him): Incredible! ☑ Amazing! ☐ Mind-blowing! ☐ Great! ☐

Overall rating (her): Joke ☐ Competent ☐ Good while it lasted ☐ Great! ☑

Contraception used: Condom ☐ Pill ☑ Morning after pill ☐ IUD ☐ Homemade ☐ None ☐

VD check-up

	Her:		Him:	
Syphilis	☐		Syphilis	☐
Gonorrhea	☐		Gonorrhea	☐
HIV	☐		HIV	☑
Genital Warts	☑		Genital Warts	☐
Herpes	☐		Herpes	☐
Thrush	☐		Thrush	☑
Chlamydia	☐		Chlamydia	☐
Ebola	☐		Ebola	☐
Other:........	☐		Other:........	☐

Who is to blame: Her ☐ Him ☐ No one ☐

☐ *We are saving ourselves for marriage and will complete this on our wedding night.* Extra questions for newly-weds: did the first time a) Live up to your expectations? Yes ☐ No ☐ b) Make you wonder what all the fuss is about? Yes ☐ No ☐ c) Make you call for an annulment? Yes ☐ No ☐

"Chemistry" Test

Drop of her blood / Drop of his blood

If mixed blood turns purple, you are a good match.
If mixed blood turns yellow, you are ill-suited.
If mixed blood stays red, test is inconclusive.

Dribble of her saliva / Dribble of his saliva

If salivas bubble briefly, you are meant to be together.
If salivas form a corrosive acid, call a doctor now.
If salivas just coalesce, test is inconclusive.

Good intentions

Are your intentions towards each other at this early stage:

Her | Dishonourable ———— Honourable ✓
Him | Dishonourable ✓ ———— Honourable

Please confirm that neither of you is secretly married with a wife and three kids or otherwise technically unavailable for a serious relationship.

Her...✓..I confirm
Him................................✓........................I confirm

Men & Women: the basics

Here is a handy reminder of the six essential differences between the sexes. Do not deviate from these facts of life or you'll end up androgynous.
1. Men hide their emotions. Women show their emotions.
2. Men want to fix problems. Women want to share problems.
3. Men like to do. Women like to talk.
4. Men are hunters. Women are gatherers.
5. Men go on looks. Women go on brains.
6. Men retreat into caves. Women read books about this.*

*Gay couples are exempt from any cave-retreating behaviour. Caves are dank, dark, and full of insects. Why on earth would anyone want to go there?

17

Saying I love you

Adopt best practice early on: tell your partner you love them every day for the rest of your relationship, and there's a good chance it will last forever. To help, we provide a reminder chart to stick on the fridge and both tick every morning as you say it.

I love you! Her ✓ Him ☐	I love you! Her ☐ Him ☐	I love you! Her ☐ Him ☐	I love you! Her ☐ Him ☐	I love you! Her ☐ Him ☐	I love you! Her ☐ Him ☐
I love you! Her ☐ Him ☐	I love you! Her ☐ Him ☐	I love you! Her ☐ Him ☐	I love you! Her ☐ Him ☐	I love you! Her ☐ Him ☐	I love you! Her ☐ Him ☐
I love you! Her ☐ Him ☐	I love you! Her ☐ Him ☐	I love you! Her ☐ Him ☐	I love you! Her ☐ Him ☐	I love you! Her ☐ Him ☐	I love you! Her ☐ Him ☐
I love you! Her ☐ Him ☐	I love you! Her ☐ Him ☐	I love you! Her ☐ Him ☐	I love you! Her ☐ Him ☐	I love you! Her ☐ Him ☐	I love you! Her ☐ Him ☐
I love you! Her ☐ Him ☐	I love you! Her ☐ Him ☐	I love you! Her ☐ Him ☐	I love you! Her ☐ Him ☐	I love you! Her ☐ Him ☐	I love you! Her ☐ Him ☐
I love you! Her ☐ Him ☐	I love you! Her ☐ Him ☐	I love you! Her ☐ Him ☐	I love you! Her ☐ Him ☐	I love you! Her ☐ Him ☐	I love you! Her ☐ Him ☐
I love you! Her ☐ Him ☐	I love you! Her ☐ Him ☐	I love you! Her ☐ Him ☐	I love you! Her ☐ Him ☐	I love you! Her ☐ Him ☐	I love you! Her ☐ Him ☐
I love you! Her ☐ Him ☐	I love you! Her ☐ Him ☐	I love you! Her ☐ Him ☐	I love you! Her ☐ Him ☐	I love you! Her ☐ Him ☐	I love you! Her ☐ Him ☐
I love you! Her ☐ Him ☐	I love you! Her ☐ Him ☐	I love you! Her ☐ Him ☐	I love you! Her ☐ Him ☐	I love you! Her ☐ Him ☐	I love you! Her ☐ Him ☐
I love you! Her ☐ Him ☐	I love you! Her ☐ Him ☐	I love you! Her ☐ Him ☐	I love you! Her ☐ Him ☐	I love you! Her ☐ Him ☐	I love you! Her ☐ Him ☐
I love you! Her ☐ Him ☐	I love you! Her ☐ Him ☐	I love you! Her ☐ Him ☐	I love you! Her ☐ Him ☐	I love you! Her ☐ Him ☐	I love you! Her ☐ Him ☐
I love you! Her ☐ Him ☐	I love you! Her ☐ Him ☐	I love you! Her ☐ Him ☐	I love you! Her ☐ Him ☐	I love you! Her ☐ Him ☐	I love you! Her ☐ Him ☐
I love you! Her ☐ Him ☐	I love you! Her ☐ Him ☐	I love you! Her ☐ Him ☐	I love you! Her ☐ Him ☐	I love you! Her ☐ Him ☐	I love you! Her ☐ Him ☐
I love you! Her ☐ Him ☐	I love you! Her ☐ Him ☐	I love you! Her ☐ Him ☐	I love you! Her ☐ Him ☐	I love you! Her ☐ Him ☐	I love you! Her ☐ Him ☐
I love you! Her ☐ Him ☐	I love you! Her ☐ Him ☐	I love you! Her ☐ Him ☐	I love you! Her ☐ Him ☐	I love you! Her ☐ Him ☐	I love you! Her ☐ Him ☐
I love you! Her ☐ Him ☐	I love you! Her ☐ Him ☐	I love you! Her ☐ Him ☐	I love you! Her ☐ Him ☐	I love you! Her ☐ Him ☐	I love you! Her ☐ Him ☐
I love you! Her ☐ Him ☐	I love you! Her ☐ Him ☐	I love you! Her ☐ Him ☐	I love you! Her ☐ Him ☐	I love you! Her ☐ Him ☐	I love you! Her ☐ Him ☐
I love you! Her ☐ Him ☐	I love you! Her ☐ Him ☐	I love you! Her ☐ Him ☐	I love you! Her ☐ Him ☐	I love you! Her ☐ Him ☐	I love you! Her ☐ Him ☐
I love you! Her ☐ Him ☐	I love you! Her ☐ Him ☐	I love you! Her ☐ Him ☐	I love you! Her ☐ Him ☐	I love you! Her ☐ Him ☐	I love you! Her ☐ Him ☐
I love you! Her ☐ Him ☐	I love you! Her ☐ Him ☐	I love you! Her ☐ Him ☐	I love you! Her ☐ Him ☐	I love you! Her ☐ Him ☐	I love you! Her ☐ Him ☐
I love you! Her ☐ Him ☐	I love you! Her ☐ Him ☐	I love you! Her ☐ Him ☐	I love you! Her ☐ Him ☐	I love you! Her ☐ Him ☐	I love you! Her ☐ Him ☐
I love you! Her ☐ Him ☐	I love you! Her ☐ Him ☐	I love you! Her ☐ Him ☐	I love you! Her ☐ Him ☐	I love you! Her ☐ Him ☐	I love you! Her ☐ Him ☐
I love you! Her ☐ Him ☐	I love you! Her ☐ Him ☐	I love you! Her ☐ Him ☐	I love you! Her ☐ Him ☐	I love you! Her ☐ Him ☐	I love you! Her ☐ Him ☐
I love you! Her ☐ Him ☐	I love you! Her ☐ Him ☐	I love you! Her ☐ Him ☐	I love you! Her ☐ Him ☐	I love you! Her ☐ Him ☐	I love you! Her ☐ Him ☐
I love you! Her ☐ Him ☐	I love you! Her ☐ Him ☐	I love you! Her ☐ Him ☐	I love you! Her ☐ Him ☐	I love you! Her ☐ Him ☐	I love you! Her ☐ Him ☐
I love you! Her ☐ Him ☐	I love you! Her ☐ Him ☐	I love you! Her ☐ Him ☐	I love you! Her ☐ Him ☐	I love you! Her ☐ Him ☐	I love you! Her ☐ Him ☐
I love you! Her ☐ Him ☐	I love you! Her ☐ Him ☐	I love you! Her ☐ Him ☐	I love you! Her ☐ Him ☐	I love you! Her ☐ Him ☐	I love you! Her ☐ Him ☐
I love you! Her ☐ Him ☐	I love you! Her ☐ Him ☐	I love you! Her ☐ Him ☐	I love you! Her ☐ Him ☐	I love you! Her ☐ Him ☐	I love you! Her ☐ Him ☐
I love you! Her ☐ Him ☐	I love you! Her ☐ Him ☐	I love you! Her ☐ Him ☐	I love you! Her ☐ Him ☐	I love you! Her ☐ Him ☐	I love you! Her ☐ Him ☐
I love you! Her ☐ Him ☐	I love you! Her ☐ Him ☐	I love you! Her ☐ Him ☐	I love you! Her ☐ Him ☐	I love you! Her ☐ Him ☐	I love you! Her ☐ Him ☐
I love you! Her ☐ Him ☐	I love you! Her ☐ Him ☐	I love you! Her ☐ Him ☐	I love you! Her ☐ Him ☐	I love you! Her ☐ Him ☐	I love you! Her ☐ Him ☐
I love you! Her ☐ Him ☐	I love you! Her ☐ Him ☐	I love you! Her ☐ Him ☐	I love you! Her ☐ Him ☐	I love you! Her ☐ Him ☐	I love you! Her ☐ Him ☐
I love you! Her ☐ Him ☐	I love you! Her ☐ Him ☐	I love you! Her ☐ Him ☐	I love you! Her ☐ Him ☐	I love you! Her ☐ Him ☐	I love you! Her ☐ Him ☐
I love you! Her ☐ Him ☐	I love you! Her ☐ Him ☐	I love you! Her ☐ Him ☐	I love you! Her ☐ Him ☐	I love you! Her ☐ Him ☐	I love you! Her ☐ Him ☐
I love you! Her ☐ Him ☐	I love you! Her ☐ Him ☐	I love you! Her ☐ Him ☐	I love you! Her ☐ Him ☐	I love you! Her ☐ Him ☐	I love you! Her ☐ Him ☐
I love you! Her ☐ Him ☐	I love you! Her ☐ Him ☐	I love you! Her ☐ Him ☐	I love you! Her ☐ Him ☐	I love you! Her ☐ Him ☐	I love you! Her ☐ Him ☐
I love you! Her ☐ Him ☐	I love you! Her ☐ Him ☐	I love you! Her ☐ Him ☐	I love you! Her ☐ Him ☐	I love you! Her ☐ Him ☐	I love you! Her ☐ Him ☐
I love you! Her ☐ Him ☐	I love you! Her ☐ Him ☐	I love you! Her ☐ Him ☐	I love you! Her ☐ Him ☐	I love you! Her ☐ Him ☐	I love you! Her ☐ Him ☐
I love you! Her ☐ Him ☐	I love you! Her ☐ Him ☐	I love you! Her ☐ Him ☐	I love you! Her ☐ Him ☐	I love you! Her ☐ Him ☐	I love you! Her ☐ Him ☐
I love you! Her ☐ Him ☐	I love you! Her ☐ Him ☐	I love you! Her ☐ Him ☐	I love you! Her ☐ Him ☐	I love you! Her ☐ Him ☐	I love you! Her ☐ Him ☐
I love you! Her ☐ Him ☐	I love you! Her ☐ Him ☐	I love you! Her ☐ Him ☐	I love you! Her ☐ Him ☐	I love you! Her ☐ Him ☐	I love you! Her ☐ Him ☐
I love you! Her ☐ Him ☐	I love you! Her ☐ Him ☐	I love you! Her ☐ Him ☐	I love you! Her ☐ Him ☐	I love you! Her ☐ Him ☐	I love you! Her ☐ Him ☐
I love you! Her ☐ Him ☐	I love you! Her ☐ Him ☐	I love you! Her ☐ Him ☐	I love you! Her ☐ Him ☐	I love you! Her ☐ Him ☐	I love you! Her ☐ Him ☐
I love you! Her ☐ Him ☐	I love you! Her ☐ Him ☐	I love you! Her ☐ Him ☐	I love you! Her ☐ Him ☐	I love you! Her ☐ Him ☐	I love you! Her ☐ Him ☐
I love you! Her ☐ Him ☐	I love you! Her ☐ Him ☐	I love you! Her ☐ Him ☐	I love you! Her ☐ Him ☐	I love you! Her ☐ Him ☐	I love you! Her ☐ Him ☐
I love you! Her ☐ Him ☐	I love you! Her ☐ Him ☐	I love you! Her ☐ Him ☐	I love you! Her ☐ Him ☐	I love you! Her ☐ Him ☐	I love you! Her ☐ Him ☐
I love you! Her ☐ Him ☐	I love you! Her ☐ Him ☐	I love you! Her ☐ Him ☐	I love you! Her ☐ Him ☐	I love you! Her ☐ Him ☐	I love you! Her ☐ Him ☐

I love you! Her □ Him □

The very first "I love you"

Date:..

Who said it:...

Reaction: "I love you too" □   Laughter □   Flight □

Choking □   Other...□

NB Only reaction A is acceptable

Our past relationships

Unless you are both extremely young, or extremely ugly, you will have had other flames. Have they turned you into a bitter and twisted emotional wreck? Deal with your baggage here once and for all, and don't let the exes drag you down.

Past relationship Hers ☐ His ☐	Past relationship Hers ☐ His ☐	Past relationship Hers ☐ His ☐
Name:................................ Age:..............	Name:................................ Age:..............	Name:................................ Age:..............
Length of the relationship:................................	Length of the relationship:................................	Length of the relationship:................................
Date of the relationship:................................	Date of the relationship:................................	Date of the relationship:................................
Reason for split:................................	Reason for split:................................	Reason for split:................................
How serious was the relationship: ..../10	How serious was the relationship: ..../10	How serious was the relationship: ..../10
How much did they mean to you: ..../10	How much did they mean to you: ..../10	How much did they mean to you: ..../10
How good were they in bed: ..../10	How good were they in bed: ..../10	How good were they in bed: ..../10
How bitter are you about them now:......../10	How bitter are you about them now:......../10	How bitter are you about them now:......../10
Do you still see them? Yes ☐ No ☐	Do you still see them? Yes ☐ No ☐	Do you still see them? Yes ☐ No ☐
Do you still fancy them? Yes* ☐ No ☐	Do you still fancy them? Yes* ☐ No ☐	Do you still fancy them? Yes* ☐ No ☐
Past relationship Hers ☐ His ☐	Past relationship Hers ☐ His ☐	Past relationship Hers ☐ His ☐
Name:................................ Age:..............	Name:................................ Age:..............	Name:................................ Age:..............
Length of the relationship:................................	Length of the relationship:................................	Length of the relationship:................................
Date of the relationship:................................	Date of the relationship:................................	Date of the relationship:................................
Reason for split:................................	Reason for split:................................	Reason for split:................................
How serious was the relationship: ..../10	How serious was the relationship: ..../10	How serious was the relationship: ..../10
How much did they mean to you: ..../10	How much did they mean to you: ..../10	How much did they mean to you: ..../10
How good were they in bed: ..../10	How good were they in bed: ..../10	How good were they in bed: ..../10
How bitter are you about them now:......../10	How bitter are you about them now:......../10	How bitter are you about them now:......../10
Do you still see them? Yes ☐ No ☐	Do you still see them? Yes ☐ No ☐	Do you still see them? Yes ☐ No ☐
Do you still fancy them? Yes* ☐ No ☐	Do you still fancy them? Yes* ☐ No ☐	Do you still fancy them? Yes* ☐ No ☐
Past relationship Hers ☐ His ☐	Past relationship Hers ☐ His ☐	Past relationship Hers ☐ His ☐
Name:................................ Age:..............	Name:................................ Age:..............	Name:................................ Age:..............
Length of the relationship:................................	Length of the relationship:................................	Length of the relationship:................................
Date of the relationship:................................	Date of the relationship:................................	Date of the relationship:................................
Reason for split:................................	Reason for split:................................	Reason for split:................................
How serious was the relationship: ..../10	How serious was the relationship: ..../10	How serious was the relationship: ..../10
How much did they mean to you: ..../10	How much did they mean to you: ..../10	How much did they mean to you: ..../10
How good were they in bed: ..../10	How good were they in bed: ..../10	How good were they in bed: ..../10
How bitter are you about them now:......../10	How bitter are you about them now:......../10	How bitter are you about them now:......../10
Do you still see them? Yes ☐ No ☐	Do you still see them? Yes ☐ No ☐	Do you still see them? Yes ☐ No ☐
Do you still fancy them? Yes* ☐ No ☐	Do you still fancy them? Yes* ☐ No ☐	Do you still fancy them? Yes* ☐ No ☐

*Proceed directly to Trouble In Paradise

I lost my virginity to   Her

Name...

Date...

I lost my virginity to   Him

Name...

Date...

Her one-night stands		Date
1		
2		
3		
4		
5		
6		
7		
8		
9		
10		
11		
12		
13		
14		
15		
16		
17		
18		
19		
20		
21		
22		
Lost count		

His one-night stands		Date
1		
2		
3		
4		
5		
6		
7		
8		
9		
10		
11		
12		
13		
14		
15		
16		
17		
18		
19		
20		
21		
22		
Lost count		

Anonymous and/or drunken encounters (estimate)

Her...

Him..

Total relationship tally

Her...

Him..

21

Poems to read together

Poetry is a well-known aphrodisiac. Strengthen your love by reading these love poems out loud together. Don't be afraid to put some real feeling into it, and make eye contact at the key romantic moments, marked by hearts.

My mistress' eyes are nothing like the sun;
Coral is far more red than her lips' red;
If snow be white, why then her breasts are dun;
If hairs be wires, black wires grow on her head.
I have seen roses damask'd, red and white,
But no such roses see I in her cheeks;
And in some perfumes is there more delight
Than in the breath that from my mistress reeks.
I love to hear her speak, yet well I know
That music hath a far more pleasing sound;
I grant I never saw a goddess go;
My mistress, when she walks, treads on the ground.
And yet, by heaven, I think my love ❤ as rare
As any she belied with false compare.

Lying asleep between the strokes of night
I saw my love lean over my sad bed,
Pale as the duskiest lily's leaf or head,
Smooth-skinned and dark, with bare throat made to bite,
Too wan for blushing and too warm for white,
But perfect-coloured without white or red.
And her lips opened amorously, and said –
I wist not what, saving one word – Delight.
And all her face was honey to my mouth,
And all her body pasture to mine eyes;
The long lithe arms and hotter hands than fire
The quivering flanks, hair smelling of the south,
The bright light feet, the splendid supple thighs
And glittering eyelids of my soul's desire ❤.

How do I love thee ❤? Let me count the ways.
I love thee to the depth and breadth and height
My soul can reach, when feeling out of sight
For the ends of Being and ideal Grace.
I love thee to the level of everyday's
Most quiet need, by sun and candle-light.
I love thee freely ❤, as men strive for Right;
I love thee purely ❤, as they turn from Praise.
I love thee with the passion put to use
In my old griefs, and with my childhood's faith.
I love thee with ❤ a love I seemed to lose
With my lost saints – I love thee with the breath,
Smiles, tears, of all my life! – and, if God choose,
I shall but love thee better after death.

Shall I compare thee to a summer's day?
Thou art more lovely and more temperate ❤.
Rough winds do shake the darling buds of May,
And summer's lease hath all too short a date.
Sometime too hot the eye of heaven shines,
And often is his gold complexion dimm'd;
And every fair from fair sometime declines,
By chance or nature's changing course untrimm'd;
But thy eternal summer shall not fade
Nor lose possession of that fair thou ow'st;
Nor shall Death brag thou wander'st in his shade,
When in eternal lines to time thou grow'st:
So long as men can breathe or eyes can see,
So long lives this, and this gives life to thee.

If thou must love me, let it be for nought
Except for love's sake only ❤. Do not say
'I love her for her smile – her look – her way
Of speaking gently – for a trick of thought
That falls in well with mine, and certes brought
A sense of pleasant ease on such a day'
For these things in themselves, Beloved, may
Be changed, or change for thee – and love, so wrought,
May be unwrought so. Neither love me for
Thine own dear pity's wiping my cheeks dry,
A creature might forget to weep, who bore
Thy comfort long, and lose thy love thereby!
But love me ❤ for love's sake, that evermore ❤
Thou may'st love on ❤, through love's eternity.

Gather ye rosebuds while ye may,
Old time is still a-flying:
And this same flower that smiles today
Tomorrow will be dying.
The glorious lamp of heaven, the sun,
The higher he's a-getting,
The sooner will his race be run,
And nearer he's to setting.
That age is best which is the first,
When youth and blood are warmer ❤,
But being spent, the worse, and worst
Times still succeed the former.
Then be not coy, but use your time,
And while ye may, go marry:
For having lost but once your prime
You may for ever tarry.

Two doves meeting in the sky ❤
Two loves hand in hand eye to eye ❤
Two parts of a loving whole ❤
Two hearts and a single soul ❤
Two stars shining big and bright ❤
Two fires bringing warmth and light ❤
Two songs played in perfect tune ❤
Two flowers growing into bloom ❤
Two doves gliding in the air ❤
Two loves free without a care ❤
Two parts of a loving whole ❤
Two hearts and a single soul ❤

She walks in beauty, like the night
Of cloudless climes and starry skies;
And all that's best of dark and bright
Meet in her aspect and her eyes:
Thus mellow'd to that tender light
Which heaven to gaudy day denies.
One shade the more, one ray the less,
Had half impair'd the nameless grace
Which waves in every raven tress,
Or softly lightens o'er her face;
Where thoughts serenely sweet express
How pure, how dear their dwelling-place ❤.
And on that cheek, and o'er that brow,
So soft, so calm, yet eloquent,
The smiles that win, the tints that glow,
But tell of days in goodness spent,
A mind at peace with all below,
A heart whose love is innocent ❤❤!

I wonder, by my troth, what thou and I
Did till we loved ❤? Were we not weaned till then?
But sucked on country pleasures childishly?
Or snorted we in the Seven Sleepers' den?
'Twas so; but this, all pleasures fancies be.
If ever any beauty I did see,
Which I desired, and got, 'twas but a dream of thee.
And now good morrow to our waking souls,
Which watch not one another out of fear;
For love all love of other sights controls,
And makes one little room an everywhere.
Let sea-discoverers to new worlds have gone,
Let maps to other, worlds on worlds have shown;
Let us possess one world, each hath one, and is one.
My face in thine eye, thine in mine appears ❤,
And true plain hearts do in the faces rest,
Where can we find two better hemispheres
Without sharp north, without declining west?
Whatever dies was not mixed equally;
If our two loves be one ❤, or thou and I
Love so alike that none do slacken, none can die.

True love is a sacred flame
That burns eternally,
And none can dim its special glow
Or change its destiny.
True love speaks in tender tones
And hears with gentle ear,
True love gives with open heart
And true love conquers fear.
True love makes no harsh demands
It neither rules nor binds,
And true love holds with gentle hands
The hearts that it entwines.

O my Luve's like a red, red rose
That's newly sprung in June ❤!
O my Luve's like the melodie
That's sweetly play'd in tune!
As fair art thou, my bonnie lass,
So deep in luve am I:
And I will luve thee still, my dear,
Till a' the seas gang dry –
Till a' the seas gang dry, my dear,
And the rocks melt wi' the sun;
I will luve thee still, my dear ❤,
While the sands o' life shall run.
And fare thee weel, my only Luve ❤!
And fare thee weel awhile!
And I will come again, my Luve ❤,
Tho' it were ten thousand mile.

What I fancy I approve,
No dislike there is in love:
Be my mistress short or tall,
And distorted therewithal:
Be she likewise one of those,
That an acre hath of nose:
Be her forehead and her eyes
Full of incongruities:
Be her cheeks so shallow too,
As to show her tongue wag through;
Be her lips ill hung or set,
And her grinders black as jet:
Hath she thin hair, hath she none,
She's to me a paragon ❤.

Where true Love burns ❤ Desire is Love's pure flame;
It is the reflex of our earthly frame,
That takes its meaning from the nobler part,
And but translates ❤ the language of the heart ❤.

Valentine's Days

With the Couple's Book, every day should be Valentine's Day. Still, there's no harm in celebrating the traditional 14th February. Make an effort to inject a little unpredictability into it though; surprise each other with a different venue, different flowers, a different compliment.

Valentine's Day 2005	Valentine's Day 2005	Valentine's Day 2005
The venue:...............................	The venue:...............................	The venue:...............................
The flowers:.............................	The flowers:.............................	The flowers:.............................
His compliment:.......................	His compliment:.......................	His compliment:.......................
His romantic performance:.........../10	His romantic performance:.........../10	His romantic performance:.........../10
Her romantic performance:.........../10	Her romantic performance:.........../10	Her romantic performance:.........../10
Overall romanticality (add scores):.........../20	Overall romanticality (add scores):.........../20	Overall romanticality (add scores):.........../20
Valentine's Day 2005	Valentine's Day 2005	Valentine's Day 2005
The venue:...............................	The venue:...............................	The venue:...............................
The flowers:.............................	The flowers:.............................	The flowers:.............................
His compliment:.......................	His compliment:.......................	His compliment:.......................
His romantic performance:.........../10	His romantic performance:.........../10	His romantic performance:.........../10
Her romantic performance:.........../10	Her romantic performance:.........../10	Her romantic performance:.........../10
Overall romanticality (add scores):.........../20	Overall romanticality (add scores):.........../20	Overall romanticality (add scores):.........../20
Valentine's Day 2005	Valentine's Day 2005	Valentine's Day 2005
The venue:...............................	The venue:...............................	The venue:...............................
The flowers:.............................	The flowers:.............................	The flowers:.............................
His compliment:.......................	His compliment:.......................	His compliment:.......................
His romantic performance:.........../10	His romantic performance:.........../10	His romantic performance:.........../10
Her romantic performance:.........../10	Her romantic performance:.........../10	Her romantic performance:.........../10
Overall romanticality (add scores):.........../20	Overall romanticality (add scores):.........../20	Overall romanticality (add scores):.........../20
Valentine's Day 2005	Valentine's Day 2005	Valentine's Day 2005
The venue:...............................	The venue:...............................	The venue:...............................
The flowers:.............................	The flowers:.............................	The flowers:.............................
His compliment:.......................	His compliment:.......................	His compliment:.......................
His romantic performance:.........../10	His romantic performance:.........../10	His romantic performance:.........../10
Her romantic performance:.........../10	Her romantic performance:.........../10	Her romantic performance:.........../10
Overall romanticality (add scores):.........../20	Overall romanticality (add scores):.........../20	Overall romanticality (add scores):.........../20

Don't look at this box until you're very old! Looking back on your lives, which was the most romantic of your Valentine's Days?.................................... Try recreating it for old times' sake, although not if it involved tumultuous sex or any kind of cardiac risk.

OUR GIFTS

There is nothing like a surprise gift to sustain the relationship! How do you pick the right one though? Avoid those dud choices by filling in our gift guide, and letting each other know the ways to your heart. ✓ = Yes, I like! ✗ = This one's a no-no!

Item	Her	Him
Flowers	☐	☐
Jewellery	☐	☐
Diamonds	☐	☐
Golf clubs	☐	☑
Toothpick	☐	☐
Hat	☐	☐
Picture of me	☐	☐
Picture of you	☐	☑
Picture of others	☐	☐
Champagne	☐	☑
Blazer	☐	☐
Sex toy	☐	☑
Sandwich	☐	☐
Marmite	☐	☐
Hamster	☐	☐
Insect	☐	☐
Soup	☐	☑
Sea anemone	☐	☐
Practical car	☐	☐
Sports car	☐	☑
Twig	☐	☐
House	☐	☑
Cash	☐	☐
Baby	☐	☐
Sexy underwear	☐	☑
Fruitbasket	☐	☐
Tie	☐	☑
Scarf	☐	☑

Item	Her	Him
Night at the opera	☐	☐
Small island	☐	☑
Employment	☐	☐
Shoes	☐	☑
DVD	☐	☐
VD	☐	☐
Musical instrument	☐	☐
Towel	☐	☐
Mug	☐	☐
Incontinence pads	☐	☐
Pizza	☐	☐
Poney	☐	☑
Kettle	☐	☐
Smoothie	☐	☐
Prize turnip	☐	☐
Trampoline	☐	☐
Trainset	☐	☐
Braces	☐	☐
Wig	☐	☐
Deodorant	☐	☐
Catsuit *for you*	☐	☑
Rolex	☐	☑
Ulcer	☐	☐
Saliva	☐	☐
Chocolates	☐	☑
Earplugs	☐	☐
Pet anteater	☐	☐
Napkin	☐	☑
Bit of the Berlin Wall	☐	☐
Motorbike	☐	☑
Tiara	☐	☑

Item	Her	Him
Sculpture of you	☐	☐
Day at the races	☐	☑
Anal intruder	☐	☐
Mouse trap	☐	☐
Pan-flute compilation	☐	☐
Teapot	☐	☐
Soft drink	☐	☐
Supermarket coupons	☐	☐
Squashed cockroach	☐	☐
Truck	☐	☐
Bird of paradise	☐	☐
Chicken nuggets	☐	☐
Ballet lessons	☐	☐
Chandelier	☐	☐
Original Rembrandt	☐	☐
Voucher for tattoo	☐	☐
Joystick	☐	☐
Soufflé	☐	☐
Drumkit	☐	☐
Stairmaster	☐	☐
Designer jeans	☐	☑
Head of rival	☐	☐
Wine (red)	☐	☑
Wine (white)	☐	☐
Wine (rosé)	☐	☐
Spare fuse	☐	☐
Umbrella	☐	☐
Stick	☐	☑
Mulch	☐	☐

Item	Her	Him
Lip gloss	☐	☐
Coal mine	☐	☐
Harp	☐	☐
Precious relic	☐	☐
Cocktail shaker	☐	☐
Junk mail	☐	☐
Cashmere sweater	☐	☐
Nuclear secret	☐	☑
Ming vase	☐	☐
Football	☐	☐
Aftershave	☐	☐
Scented candle	☐	☐
Empty beer can	☐	☐
Meat	☐	☐
Bone china	☐	☐
Dinosaur bone	☐	☐
Dog bone	☐	☐
Electron	☐	☐
Wiener schnitzel	☐	☐
Consumer good	☐	☐
Three-piece suit	☐	☐
Sex change	☐	☐
Insurance policy	☐	☐
Saddle	☐	☑
Cufflinks	☐	☑
Brown sugar	☐	☐
Trip of a lifetime	☐	☑
WMD	☐	☐
Holy Grail	☐	☑
Shampoo	☐	☐

Item	Her	Him
High heels	☐	☐
Poem	☐	☐
Poem about you	☐	☐
Poem about me	☐	☐
Rare orchid	☐	☐
Original sputnik	☐	☐
Joke apron	☐	☐
Baseball cap	☐	☐
Hope	☐	☐
Massage	☐	☐
Manicure	☐	☐
Pedicure	☐	☐
Baby dolphin	☐	☐
Brain transplant	☐	☑
Caviar	☐	☐
Pretty ribbon	☐	☐
Birthday cake	☐	☐
Ice cream	☐	☑
Apple pie	☐	☑
World peace	☐	☐
Shaving kit	☐	☐
Gondola ride	☐	☐
Parachute	☐	☑
Cookies	☐	☐
Decanter	☐	☑
Power drill	☐	☑
False teeth	☐	☐
Burger	☐	☐
Book	☐	☑
Book by Benrik	☑	☑

Handy shopping reminder

His shirt size 14½ 15 15½ 16 16½ 17 17½

His waist size 30 32 34 36 38 40

His shoe size 6 7 8 9 10 11 12

Her dress size 8 10 12 14 16 18 20

Her bra size 28 30 32 34 36 38 40

Her cup size A B C D DD F G

Her shoe size 3 4 5 6 7 8 9

Our Flowers

Circle the flowers you are happy to receive.

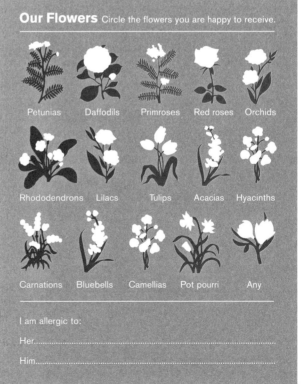

Petunias   Daffodils   Primroses   Red roses   Orchids

Rhododendrons   Lilacs   Tulips   Acacias   Hyacinths

Carnations   Bluebells   Camellias   Pot pourri   Any

I am allergic to:

Her...

Him...

Meeting the parents

This is a minefield for both of you. All it takes is one careless slip and months of preparation can go down the drain. Plot your moves carefully using this floor plan and the accompanying small-talk tips. Don't worry, your parents are as nervous as you.

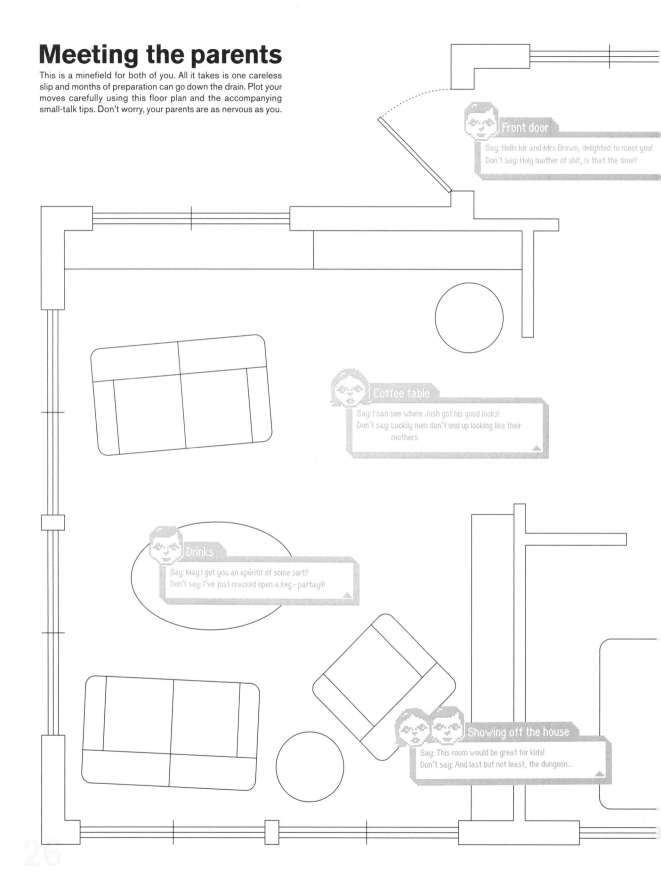

Front door
Say: Hello Mr and Mrs Brown, delighted to meet you!
Don't say: Holy mother of shit, is that the time?

Coffee table
Say: I can see where Josh got his good looks!
Don't say: Luckily men don't end up looking like their mothers.

Drinks
Say: May I get you an apéritif of some sort?
Don't say: I've just cracked open a keg - partay!!!

Showing off the house
Say: This room would be great for kids!
Don't say: And last but not least, the dungeon...

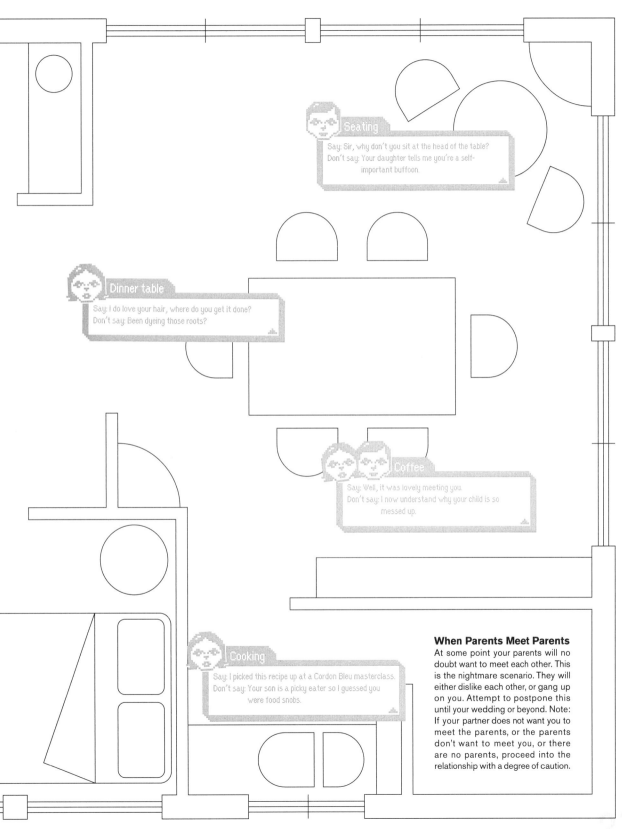

Seating
Say: Sir, why don't you sit at the head of the table?
Don't say: Your daughter tells me you're a self-important buffoon.

Dinner table
Say: I do love your hair, where do you get it done?
Don't say: Been dyeing those roots?

Coffee
Say: Well, it was lovely meeting you.
Don't say: I now understand why your child is so messed up.

Cooking
Say: I picked this recipe up at a Cordon Bleu masterclass.
Don't say: Your son is a picky eater so I guessed you were food snobs.

When Parents Meet Parents
At some point your parents will no doubt want to meet each other. This is the nightmare scenario. They will either dislike each other, or gang up on you. Attempt to postpone this until your wedding or beyond. Note: If your partner does not want you to meet the parents, or the parents don't want to meet you, or there are no parents, proceed into the relationship with a degree of caution.

Parental feedback

Parents: these are your pages. Here you get to air your thoughts on the latest brute/slut to gatecrash their way into your little angel's heart. Remember though: they may not be good enough for your precious darling offspring, but they too have feelings.

Her father

Questions to ask yourself: Is this fellow a suitable match for my daughter? Are his intentions honourable? What is his earning potential?

....

....

....

....

....

....

....

....

....

....I give this relationship my blessing Yes ☐ No ☐

His father

Questions to ask yourself: Is she pretty? Has the boy done good? Or is she going to eat him for breakfast?..

....

....

....

....

....

....

....

....

....I give this relationship my blessing Yes ☐ No ☐

Her mother

Questions to ask yourself: Is he a nice young man? Does he love her? Will he take care of her? Or will he merely take advantage?.........................

....

....

....

....

....

....

....

....

....

....I give this relationship my blessing Yes ☐ No ☐

His mother

Questions to ask yourself: Who is this hussy? Who does she think she is? She's not good enough! Why can't my boy see through her? Oh he's

so young! Jezebel!!! Where's that kitchen knife?...

....

....

....

....

....

....

....

....

....

....

....

....

....

....

....

....

....

....

....

....

....I give this relationship my blessing No ☐ No ☐

What the stars say about us

Is your love story written in the stars? Use this Benrik astrological compatibility chart to determine whether you are meant to burn bright or doomed to implode. It's not totally scientific of course, but it's still 97% accurate.

	Aries	Taurus	Gemini	Cancer	Leo	Virgo
Aries	You will have a great time together and love each other till death tears you apart. 9/9	Taurus will have a great time but Aries will be mostly repressed and miserable. 3/9	Gemini and Aries are the perfect combination astrologically, if they abstain from sex. 4/9	Cancer will stay at home minding the kids while Aries enjoys affairs on business trips.	Leo and Aries will enjoy kinky sex for 3 weeks then realize it's not a long-term thing. 2/9	Aries will drive Virgo to divorce within si[x] months, then sue them for alimony. 1/
Taurus	Taurus will have a great time but Aries will be mostly repressed and miserable. 3/9	The Taurus combo is a winner. Whatever life throws at them, they will survive. 9/9	Gemini is a little money grabber. Taurus should be careful, or face total ruin. 3/9	Taurus and Cancer will get on if they marry on a sunny day. If not, all hell will break loose. 5/9	Leo and Taurus are a big no-no. 0/9	Virgo is in for a surprise when Taurus reveals the existence of a seconde spouse still in jail. 2/
Gemini	Gemini and Aries are the perfect combination astrologically, if they abstain from sex. 4/9	Gemini is a little money grabber. Taurus should be careful, or face total ruin. 3/9	Gemini and Gemini can work out, as long as Gemini doesn't try to steal the limelight. 3/9	Cancer wants to settle down. Gemini just wants to partay-partay! Forget about this one. 1/9	Leo and Gemini will marry, have a beautiful baby boy, and become rich as Croesus. 9/9	Gemini will eventually leave Virgo after he finds out about that affair with Sagittarius. 2/
Cancer	Cancer will stay at home minding the kids while Aries enjoys affairs on business trips. 2/9	Taurus and Cancer will get on if they marry on a sunny day. If not, all hell will break loose. 5/9	Cancer wants to settle down. Gemini just wants to partay-partay! Forget about this one. 1/9	Cancer / Cancer could work, as after all they're the same sign and should be similar.	Leo and Cancer will try out all sorts of filthy stuff that could get them arrested in Utah. 6/9	Virgo is far too good for Cancer, how they got together is a real mystery. 1/
Leo	Leo and Aries will enjoy kinky sex for 3 weeks then realize it's not a long-term thing.	Leo and Taurus are a big no-no. 0/9	Leo and Gemini will marry, have a beautiful baby boy, and become rich as Croesus. 9/9	Leo and Cancer will try out all sorts of filthy stuff that could get them arrested in Utah. 6/9	Leo couples will devour each other!!! Not really, but it's a compulsory astrology joke.	Virgo and Leo can be happy, but will always secretly feel that they've not met "the one". 5/
Virgo	Aries will drive Virgo to divorce within six months, then sue them for alimony. 1/9	Virgo is in for a surprise when Taurus reveals the existence of a second spouse still in jail. 2/9	Gemini will eventually leave Virgo after he finds out about that affair with Sagittarius. 2/9	Virgo is far too good for Cancer, how they got together is a real mystery. 1/9	Virgo and Leo can be happy, but will always secretly feel that they've not met "the one". 5/9	Virgo and Virgo are the perfect couple, destined to live and love happil[y] ever after. 9/
Libra	Libra and Aries are opposites in love. This is supposed to be a good thing somehow. 7/9	Taurus and Libra will fall madly in love and have 4 children, one of whom will become rich. 8/9	Libra and Gemini's love will burn so bright that a musical will be written about it. 9/9	Cancer and Libra? You stand more of a chance than Cancer / Gemini. Those losers! 4/9	Leo and Libra will divorce messily, with Libra getting the beach house. 2/9	Libra and Virgo wi[ll] marry and stay togethe[r] but mainly for the sake o[f] the kids. 4/
Scorpio	These two signs will enjoy playing chamber music together, but not much else. 5/9	If Scorpio and Taurus get together, the whole planet will be in danger. Try to prevent this. 0/9	These two will form a lovely couple once he has conquered his fear of French kissing. 7/9	Scorpio and Cancer are living testimony to the power of love. Keep it up guys. 9/9	Scorpio's drinking will plague this relationship. Are you married to Leo or to the bottle?!? 1/9	Virgo and Scorpio are in love, but can't seem to stay faithful, no one can work out why. 2/
Sagittarius	Sagittarius and Aries will win the admiration of all in their community for their love. 9/9	The sex will be great for the first 2 years, then will lapse into routine and eventually stop. 2/9	Gemini and Sagittarius will be fine but only if they don't believe in horoscopes. 2/9	Sagittarius is a dirty dirty whore! How could you do that to nice Cancer? Shame on you. 1/9	Sagittarius and Leo get on so well other couples will feel insecure and start avoiding them. 7/9	Sagittarius has loved Virgo from day 1, bu[t] never dares to ask them out. 8/
Capricorn	Aries is too headstrong for Capricorn! Don't go there Capricorn! 2/9	Capricorn and Taurus are very compatible in love. Their kids will be ugly though. 5/9	This is a safe bet, though you won't really light each other's fires. But that's life. 7/9	You are well-suited, but Capricorn will become irrationally jealous of Cancer's secretary. 6/9	Leo and Capricorn end it because Capricorn just refuses to admit losing the car keys! 4/9	You will annoy each other so much that both your sexual orientations will change. 3/
Aquarius	Aquarius and Aries make great lovers, especially if they are (both) homosexual. 8/9	Aquarius is too selfish to listen to Taurus's very real complaints about the housework. 4/9	Aquarius and Gemini can look forward to a life full of romance, flowers and chocolates. 9/9	These two get on each other's nerves, it's just one of those things. 1/9	Aquarius and Leo don't really like each other, but are both into outdoor sex big time. 4/9	Aquarius and Virgo date, marry, buy [a] house, have 2.4 kids and die happy. 9/
Pisces	Pisces will smother Aries with love to the point where Aries just needs some fuckin' space. 3/9	There are no recorded cases of these two being together, so we simply don't know. –	Pisces and Gemini can look forward to a life full of complaints, petty grudges and bills. 2/9	Pisces and Cancer can't keep their hands off each other, frankly it's embarrassing. 8/9	Pisces is drawn to Leo's magnetic charm. Leo is drawn to Pisces's family fortune. 8/9	Pisces and Virgo would have got on just fine, only they hadn't bough[t] this book. 6/

	Libra	Scorpio	Sagittarius	Capricorn	Aquarius	Pisces
Aries	Libra and Aries are opposites in love. This is supposed to be a good thing somehow. 7/9	These two signs will enjoy playing chamber music together, but not much else. 5/9	Sagittarius and Aries will win the admiration of all in their community for their love. 9/9	Aries is too headstrong for Capricorn! Don't go there Capricorn! 2/9	Aquarius and Aries make great lovers, especially if they are (both) homosexual. 8/9	Pisces will smother Aries with love to the point where Aries just needs some fuckin' space! 3/9
Taurus	Taurus and Libra will fall madly in love and have 4 children, one of whom will become rich. 8/9	If Scorpio and Taurus get together, the whole planet will be in danger. Try to prevent this. 0/9	The sex will be great for the first 2 years, then will lapse into routine and eventually stop. 2/9	Capricorn and Taurus are very compatible in love. Their kids will be ugly though. 2/9	Aquarius is too selfish to listen to Taurus's very real complaints about the housework. 4/9	There are no recorded cases of these two being together, so we simply don't know. –
Gemini	Libra and Gemini's love will burn so bright that a musical will be written about it. 9/9	These two will form a lovely couple once he has conquered his fear of French kissing. 7/9	Gemini and Sagittarius will be fine but only if they don't believe in horoscopes. 2/9	This is a safe bet, though you won't really light each other's fires. But that's life. 7/9	Aquarius and Gemini can look forward to a life full of romance, flowers and chocolates. 9/9	Pisces and Gemini can look forward to a life full of complaints, petty grudges and bills. 2/9
Cancer	Cancer and Libra? You stand more of a chance than Cancer / Gemini. Those losers! 4/9	Scorpio and Cancer are living testimony to the power of love. Keep it up guys. 9/9	Sagittarius is a dirty dirty whore! How could you do that to nice Cancer? Shame on you. 1/9	You are well-suited, but Capricorn will become irrationally jealous of Cancer's secretary. 6/9	These two get on each other's nerves, it's just one of those things. 1/9	Pisces and Cancer can't keep their hands off each other, frankly it's embarrassing. 8/9
Leo	Leo and Libra will divorce messily, with Libra getting the beach house. 2/9	Scorpio's drinking will plague this relationship. Are you married to Leo or to the bottle?!? 1/9	Sagittarius and Leo get on so well other couples will feel insecure and start avoiding them. 7/9	Leo and Capricorn end it because Capricorn just refuses to admit losing the car keys! 4/9	Aquarius and Leo don't really like each other, but are both into outdoor sex big time. 8/9	Pisces is drawn to Leo's magnetic charm. Leo is drawn to Pisces's family fortune. 8/9
Virgo	Libra and Virgo will marry and stay together, but mainly for the sake of the kids. 4/9	Virgo and Scorpio are in love, but can't seem to stay faithful, no one can work out why. 2/9	Sagittarius has loved Virgo from day 1, but never dares to ask them out. 8/9	You will annoy each other so much that both your sexual orientations will change.	Aquarius and Virgo will date, marry, buy a house, have 2.4 kids, and die happy. 9/9	Pisces and Virgo would have got on just fine, if only they hadn't bought this book. 6/9
Libra	Libra & Libra will have a lucrative career in porn if they surmount their chronic shyness. 6/9	Scorpio will toy with Libra before discarding them like a crumpled kleenex. Heartless. 3/9	The two of you are made for each other! Oh no sorry, that's Virgo and Virgo, not you. 1/9	Libra and Capricorn will marry, but Capricorn is tame in bed and so Libra will sleep around. 3/9	Aquarius and Libra try to make it work, but their relationship counsellor is useless. 4/9	Pisces will only marry Libra after they pretend to be Leo. But you can't cheat the stars! 3/9
Scorpio	Scorpio will toy with Libra before discarding them like a crumpled kleenex. Heartless. 3/9	A successful Scorpio double act is rare but possible. These two will breed like rabbits! 8/9	Sagittarius and Scorpio are so much in love that everyone who meets them goes "aah…" 2/9	Capricorn and Scorpio can last a lifetime, but not if he keeps leaving the toilet seat up. 5/9	Insatiable appetites. They keep pestering their acquaintances for threesomes. 5/9	Scorpio will make rude comments about Pisces in front of others. Pisces will leave. 1/9
Sagittarius	The two of you are made for each other! Oh no sorry, that's Virgo and Virgo, not you. 1/9	Sagittarius and Scorpio are so much in love that everyone who meets them goes "aah…" 2/9	Sagittarius / Sagittarius is an OK combination, even if it doesn't exactly roll off the tongue. 6/9	Capricorn / Sagittarius will axe-murder each other over something petty like the dog. 0/9	You will enjoy a torrid illicit affair, but get found out through your credit card statements. 5/9	Sagittarius and Pisces fancy each other, only they don't realize it. 1/9
Capricorn	Libra and Capricorn will marry, but Capricorn is tame in bed and so Libra will sleep around. 3/9	Capricorn and Scorpio can last a lifetime, but not if he keeps leaving the toilet seat up. 5/9	Capricorn / Sagittarius will axe-murder each other over something petty like the dog. 0/9	Capricorn/Capricorn are just too different to get on. 3/9	Aquarius and Capricorn are best friends and lovers! Lucky them! 6/9	Pisces and Capricorn are natural soulmates and will love each other very very much. 9/9
Aquarius	Aquarius and Libra try to make it work, but their relationship counsellor is useless. 4/9	Insatiable appetites. They keep pestering their acquaintances for threesomes. 5/9	You will enjoy a torrid illicit affair, but get found out through your credit card statements. 5/9	Aquarius and Capricorn are best friends and lovers! Lucky them! 6/9	Aquarius and Aquarius will fight and fight but have angry "let's make up" sex afterwards. 4/9	Pisces / Aquarius are in love but Pisces will put all their savings on a horse and lose. 6/9
Pisces	Pisces will only marry Libra after they pretend to be Leo. But you can't cheat the stars! 3/9	Scorpio will make rude comments about Pisces in front of others. Pisces will leave. 1/9	Sagittarius and Pisces fancy each other, only they don't realize it. 1/9	Pisces and Capricorn are natural soulmates and will love each other very very much. 9/9	Pisces / Aquarius are in love but Pisces will put all their savings on a horse and lose. 6/9	Pisces and Pisces will last forever and ever, but only if they purchase this book. 9/9

Missing you

Much as you may feel you've been joined at the hip, there will come times when you must part. This page is for the one left behind nursing the open wound that is your temporary separation.

Stick lock of his hair here

Stick lock of his pubic hair here

Spray his aftershave here

Write his name 100 times here

1.................................	26.................................	51.................................	76.................................
2.................................	27.................................	52.................................	77.................................
3.................................	28.................................	53.................................	78.................................
4.................................	29.................................	54.................................	79.................................
5.................................	30.................................	55.................................	80.................................
6.................................	31.................................	56.................................	81.................................
7.................................	32.................................	57.................................	82.................................
8.................................	33.................................	58.................................	83.................................
9.................................	34.................................	59.................................	84.................................
10................................	35................................	60................................	85................................
11................................	36................................	61................................	86................................
12................................	37................................	62................................	87................................
13................................	38................................	63................................	88................................
14................................	39................................	64................................	89................................
15................................	40................................	65................................	90................................
16................................	41................................	66................................	91................................
17................................	42................................	67................................	92................................
18................................	43................................	68................................	93................................
19................................	44................................	69................................	94................................
20................................	45................................	70................................	95................................
21................................	46................................	71................................	96................................
22................................	47................................	72................................	97................................
23................................	48................................	73................................	98................................
24................................	49................................	74................................	99................................
25................................	50................................	75................................	100...............................

Count down the minutes until you see him again

60	59	58	57	56	55	54	53	52	51	50	49	48	47
46	45	44	43	42	41	40	39	38	37	36	35	34	33
32	31	30	29	28	27	26	25	24	23	22	21	20	19
18	17	16	15	14	13	12	11	10	9	8	7	6	5	4	3	2	1

Weep here until his return

Telepathy You would miss the other less if you could read their thoughts wherever they were. Develop your telepathic abilities with this easy exercise. Practise sending and receiving in turn. The sender should hold the book on their lap. The receiver should sit at the other end of the room, back turned. The sender points to one of the two symbols here (empty heart/full heart) and then tries to communicate it mentally to the receiver. When the sender is focused, he or she says: ready. The receiver must then use their mental powers to interpret the signal. Record their guess and check it against the correct answer. At first, the results may be inconclusive, but do this 200 times a day for six months to a year, and you will almost definitely see results.

Empty heart   Full heart

Stick lock of her hair here

Stick lock of her pubic hair here

Spray her perfume here

Write her name 100 times here

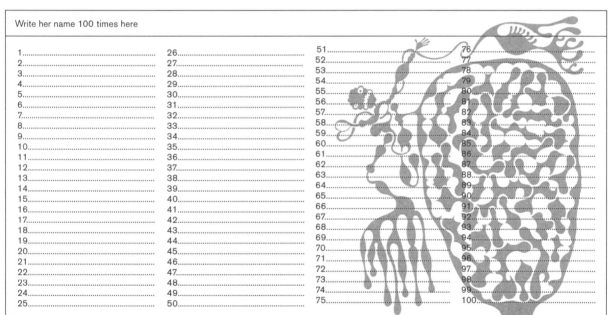

1........................	26........................	51........................	76........
2........................	27........................	52........................	77........
3........................	28........................	53........................	78........
4........................	29........................	54........................	79........
5........................	30........................	55........................	80........
6........................	31........................	56........................	81........
7........................	32........................	57........................	82........
8........................	33........................	58........................	83........
9........................	34........................	59........................	84........
10........................	35........................	60........................	85........
11........................	36........................	61........................	86........
12........................	37........................	62........................	87........
13........................	38........................	63........................	88........
14........................	39........................	64........................	89........
15........................	40........................	65........................	90........
16........................	41........................	66........................	91........
17........................	42........................	67........................	92........
18........................	43........................	68........................	93........
19........................	44........................	69........................	94........
20........................	45........................	70........................	95........
21........................	46........................	71........................	96........
22........................	47........................	72........................	97........
23........................	48........................	73........................	98........
24........................	49........................	74........................	99........
25........................	50........................	75........................	100........

Count down the minutes until you see her again

60	**59**	**58**	**57**	**56**	**55**	**54**	**53**	**52**	**51**	**50**	**49**	**48**	**47**
46	**45**	**44**	**43**	**42**	**41**	**40**	**39**	**38**	**37**	**36**	**35**	**34**	**33**
32	**31**	**30**	**29**	**28**	**27**	**26**	**25**	**24**	**23**	**22**	**21**	**20**	**19**
18	**17**	**16**	**15**	**14**	**13**	**12**	**11**	**10**	**9**	**8**	**7**	**6**	**5**	**4**	**3**	**2**	**1**

Weep here until her return

33

The Couple's Book — Teenage Special

Hiya! Alright? If you're "teens", this bit's for you. we know it's not easy sometimes at your age, cuz of parents and school and stuff. your bodies are changin' and there's not a lot you can do 'bout it. But read on and we'll help you get a grip on the greasy little hormones coursing through your spindly bodies. wicked.

BOY

name...age...........................

nickname..

favourite subject...

favourite teacher...

what you wanna be when you grow up: popstar ☐ TV presenter ☐

footballer ☐ other (specify)..☐

Ladee

name...age...........................

nickname..

favourite subject...

favourite teacher...

what you wanna be when you grow up: popstar ☐ TV presenter ☐

supermodel ☐ other (specify)......................................☐

practise your dream teenage tattoo here

where did you hook up?!?

school	☐
shopping mall	☐
Disco	☐
friend's house	☐
bus stop	☐
carpark	☐
other	☐

Who pulled who?!?...pulled.........................

Did you fancy each other?!? like mad ☐ like crazy ☐ like hell ☐
Is he a hottie?!? yes ☐ no ☐ occasionally ☐
Is she a hottie?!? yes ☐ no ☐ occasionally ☐
Is he fit?!? yes ☐ no ☐ occasionally ☐
Is she fit?!? yes ☐ no ☐ occasionally ☐

french-kissing: an expert guide
Approchez vous de votre partenaire et embrassez le ou la doucement, levres a peine ecartees. Puis, fermez les yeux, laissez glisser votre langue dans sa bouche entrouverte, et lechez langoureusement le pourtour de ses gencives. Gemissez de temps en temps, de facon a communiquer votre plaisir, si votre partenaire reagit positivement, poussez carrement votre langue a fond dans sa bouche, lui chatouillant presque la glotte. profitez de l'effet de surprise pour lui caresser le derriere. Le baiser ne prend fin que lorsqu'il ou elle s'evanouit de bonheur.

34

our favourite band ever!

week 1...
week 2...
week 3...
week 4...
week 5...
week 6...
week 7...
week 8...
week 9...
week 10...
week 11...
week 12...

pet names for each other! here is a selection of permissible
pet names. tick your choice (max. 3) or come up with your own.

honey ☐	sweetheart ☐	princess ☐	angel ☐	babe ☐
baby ☐	honeybunch ☐	cheri ☐	kitten ☐	boo ☐
darling ☐	precious ☐	cupcake ☐	doll ☐	ho ☐
sweetie ☐	sweetie pie ☐	bunny ☐	sexy ☐	tiger ☐
big boy ☐	gorgeous ☐	hotstuff ☐	cutie ☐	bitch ☐
hotlips ☐	sunshine ☐	nacho ☐	muffin ☐	killer ☐

other:..
....
....

**The first
time for teens**

Have you had sex for the first time yet? Yes ☐ No ☐

If yes, how bad was it?
Bad ☐ Embarrassingly bad ☐ Excruciatingly bad ☐

How long did he last? ....seconds

Were you relieved to have lost your virginity? Yes ☐ No ☐

Did you tell all your friends about it?
Her   Yes ☐ No ☐
Him   Immediately ☐ The next day ☐

Has this first experience traumatized you to the point
where you anticipate needing therapy to overcome it
in later life? Yes ☐ No ☐
If yes, how many hours................................(estimate)

Remember! The legal age of consent is 21.

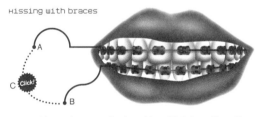

kissing with braces

braces these days are designed to click together, thus
facilitating tongue kissing. getting them to lock
together may take a bit of practice, but you will be
richly rewarded for your efforts. see our diagram for
help, or speak to your orthodontist. coolio.

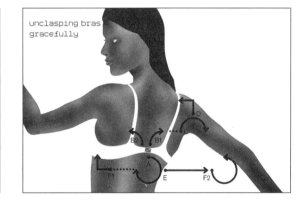

unclasping bras
gracefully

the secret meaning of spots

spots on the cheeks: you're a teenager
spots on the forehead: your brain
    is finally growing
spots on the nose: you're an attention-seeker
spots everywhere: no sex for you quite yet
spot on the lip: that's not a spot, that's herpes

Blacklist

These individuals have behaved badly in the past, treating lovers with contempt. It is with a heavy heart that we name and shame them here, thereby damaging their chances of finding a partner. But they should really have thought of it earlier, before tangling with people's feelings.*

Anna Rogan
Lottie Desmond
Mark McLaughlin
Matthew Tan
Luke Chase
John Nightingale
Paul Sands
Simon Kay
Miriam Rosen
Nancy Partington
Erica Winston
Sophie Church
Lily Samuel
Lauren Adams
Ben Richardson
Darren Linley
Jacob Holden
Elliot Mason
Trevor Hayes
Anthony Underwood
Nicolas Brant
Catherine Fordham
Jessica Davies
Lucas Mires
Josh Drew
Gary Amberly
Ian Bowes
Katie Coleman
Amanda Jones
Alexander Wright
Daniel Gibson
Adam Nicols
Jamie Kennedy
Gavin Watling
Mike Smith
Jenny Lindhill
Miranda Carpenter
Barry Elson
Chris Fitzgerald
Daphne Enfield
Pearl Long
Neil Buttle
Jolie Kashkall
Anne-Marie Payne

Bill Beaumont
Tony Loughton
Jack Beechwood
Mick Hawk
Brad Michaels
Jason Purdy
Rebecca Milton
Anne Burrell
Andrea Fox
Deborah Tanguy
Beverley Davids
Carl Cannonbury
Christopher Maple
Charlotte Black
Claudia Stroud
Penny Midhurst
Edward Leighton
Dominic Wood
James Ellis
Tom Wade
Thomas Baker
Elizabeth Burvill
Ellen Davids
Emma Manana
Edmund Rainfray
Gareth Aitchison
Emile Hickman
Edgar Burrows
Rachel Yarker
Ralph Skinner
Scott Blackstock
Phillip Shearer
Susan Solomon
Vincent Pieri
Vickie Mollison
Nina Moore
Tania Day
Joanne Meyer
Roger Dodson
Kerry Chavez
Julia Billings
Victor Padilla
Alexis Pitt
Francis Jordan

Bruno Da Silva
Carmen Schneider
Betty Lusk
Margery Pickworth
Rob Overton
Robin Honrath
Jerry Gilmore
Russ Hatch
Dennis Copeland
Mary Schmidt
Isabelle Hollis
Thomas Zimmerman
Berny Cowan
Emily Horner
Sola Blanchard
Jenna Lackey
Rosie Hall
Liz Burks
Emile Willis
Rosie Cahill
Yvonne Taylor
Isaiah Black
Gretchen Gaunt
Sophie Melton
Alison Baez
Laura Champion
Alain Rosas
John Gaston
Tamara Bradford
Yael Cohen
Jared Lyford
Brett Goldman
Ken Dodson
Al Hooks
Justin Tanner
Rebecca Lovell
EddieGaskell
Kim Moyce
Damien Levison
Michel Dupoux
Chloe Logan
Cecilia Jessop
Estelle Bardon
Prue Alcott

Naomi Davidson
Clare Ward
Irma Garland
Ben Atkinson
Ben McCann
Jamie Kane
Alan Bridges
Eva Holland
Todd Burris
Edward Gregory
Rachel Stagner
Cynthia Singleton
Pam Rosado
George Bon
Tara Dillon
Pete Hudson
Jonas Boone
Sonya Valencia
Marion Kay
Effie Desai
Jill Galindo
Steven Munoz
Rachel Watkinson
Anabelle McCord
Isaac Kinsey
Jason Linwood
Clinton Myerson
Tish Messer
Vicky Page
Denise Mardon
Iris Hart
Tracy Bledsoe
Gail McCollum
Donna McNeill
Richard Irwin
Ricky Snyder
Roger Farrell
Caroline Block
Craig Salvador
Jesus Fernandez
Donny Knowles
Brad Stapleton
Darren Benson
Tim Wade

Ronnie Gaines
Reg Kelly
Jackie Robbins
Seth Kinney
Ali Pierce
Tiffany Albert
Sofia Vitez
Diane Lehman
James McFarlane
Joseph Gainsley
Jerry Cunningham
Marcus Davitte
Louise Ham
Albert Harpoole
Aymeric Pineda
Richie Mendoza
Barbara Asquith
Bryan Buckle
Salvatore Diaz
Terry Wells
Sam Larkin
Francois Dumas
Lisa Blair
Randal Coleman
Lawrence Horn
Donald Talbot
Caroline French
Keith Fulton
Monica Perry
Karen Amos
Daisy Coles
Octavia Gabriel
Cassie Bloom
Marco Chandler
Christie Gabriel
Brian Lowe
David Robles
Dan Velazquez
Curtis Mckinney
Alexis Brine
Shannon Krause
Kevin Simpson
Abraham Hewitt
Tony Gordon

Lois Bridgmont
Lloyd Noel
Kathy Berger
Rob Trejo
Esther Atkins
Chris McKinley
Gerald Voss
Chad Benton
Mary Hayes
Sylvie Corbett
Jose Guerrero
Edith Dunleavy
Brian Forrest
Erin McLaughlin
Jess Kinney
Helga Joyce
Ashley Pack
Nicole Clarke
Jeffrey Frank
Kelsey Lunsford
Juliette Ashmore
Sarah Rollins
Travis Chung
Troy Ballard
Lorenzo Ballard
Justin Witt
Darren Boone
Karen Yarborough
Michael Larsen
Orlando Berry
Julian Ashton
Wilma Katz
Fred Joyner
Amanda Hunter
Matt Presley
Denise Marsh
Tom Holbrook
Kelly Palacios
Hugo Napier
Greg Metcalf
Eddie Shepherd
Angela Mercer
Juliet Page
Halle McQueen

36

Will Mitchell	Rachel Davey	Caroline Palmer	Kai Steele	Thomas Austin	Luke Dickinson
Aubrey Boone	Ernest Osmond	Albert Wells	Rachid Abdul	Kristi McNamara	Reuben Welch
Rowena Wilkes	Ashley Manning	Alexander Chan	Susie Johnson	Colette Jospin	Ilene Medrano
Edmundo Hernandez	Anita Phelps	Caitlin Brennan	Max Crane	Samuel Attwood	Matthew Norris
Simon Branch	Emily Kenny	Silas Hyatt	Perla Munoz	Natalie Gandolfi	Matthew Steiner
Jeffery Gustafson	Michael Moorehead	Kim Bourgeois	Benny Davenport	Diana Burks	Lorrie Bliss
Janine Larkin	Danny Hudson	Andrew Larkin	Fanny Dalton	Renee Pruitt	Maria Stapleton
Roberta Lyon	Meredith Holford	Andrea Mayberry	Geoff Custantin	Amelia Carlson	Bridget Herron
Sally Rainey	Duncan Etheridge	Esther Medina	Anita Morin	Seth Miner	Barbara Elias
Rosalind Atkin	Oliver Mendez	Sean Wilcox	Kylie Emery	Carol Shapiro	Herbert Palmer
Kyle Todd	Bernard Salmon	Hannah Newton	Henry Shields	Michel Audry	Ricardo Vega
Darius Scott	Denis Polani	Simon Caldwell	Lara Dennison	Ray Alexander	Jay Akins
Armand Scot	Lauren Turner	Will Pena	Fabian Judie	Juliette Hooks	Rolando Huerta
Lizzie McDonald	Stefan Goldman	Juan Mercado	Guy Mead	Katherine Lacy	Ashley Routledge
Frances Gore	Diane Hammer	Estelle Wilkinson	Elaine Ryan	Shailesh Patel	Jean-Marie Leblanc
Eric Mohr	Raphael Dobson	Antonia Woodbridge	Stewart Werner	Vanessa Downey	Jared Couch
Chris Madden	John Sheppard	Tara Newbury	Angelina Correro	Katy Creed	Imelda Chavez
Luke Muddleston	Patrick Whittaker	Dave Hambey	Tammy Daley	Sean Tolbert	Nathaniel Moss
Rich Hackett	Ian Fitzpatrick	Teresa Carter	Nick Hooker	Federico Gonzalez	Beth Roman
Dina Rosario	Rachel Jamieson	Robin Mendoza	Susan Keener	Florence Galloway	Sabrina Fowler
Octavio Marco	Nathan McCall	Mallory Hubbard	Hans Schurings	Doug Beaver	Hector Cornell
Ros Coates	Brandon Hayward	Amy Carter-Foss	Adrian Burnett	Marlene Neal	Larry Borden
Sylvia Da Rubio	Felix Maurier	Karla Drake	Mike Roman	Stella Briner	Duncan Cassidy
Betty Velasquez	Dominic Meyer	Walt Bainford	Al Brindlow	Kate Boersk	Tatiana Johnson
Tiffany Coates	Cindy Allison	Aurelia Villanueva	Clara Holder	Cliff Huffsttrom	Leslie-Ann Russell
Shirley Planer	Virginia Proctor	Olivia Battista	Betsy Coker	Deanne McCauley	Kim Askew
Brad Hutchinson	Pete Harrell	Zack Rainer	Hattie Crossland	Luciano Landri	Aimee Lundy
Myrtle Sanchez	Kirk Rosales	Charlie Ragland	Melissa Padge	Diego Wilkins	Edgar Page
Ingrid Andersson	Emmanuel Gold	Alfred Dixon	Ted Vicente	Jeremy Rock	Sergio Clark
Maria Beltrano	Aaron Koons	Alex Welsh	Bert Nealy	Elisha Richey	Jeremiah Lutz
Rodriguo Martinez	Vincent Slater	Sheila Downing	Aileen Johnson	Claudia Goulding	Jasper Gregson
Stevie Osborne	Keith Tanner	Stacy Bishop	Barry Glanville	Tyra Hull	Naomi Cunningham
Heather Frey	Ben McKee	Laura Weiss	Norma Feldman	Christy Sanford	Tommy Lugo
Suzanne Ballard	Julia Carey	Elliott Batchelor	Cedric Dill	Pat Friedkin	Ivana Deal
Ruth Gregory	Amy Tripp	Kristian Rasmussen	Kitty Beale	Jenny McGee	Valerie Moreno
Rina Alfaro	Sarah Arnold	Liana Craig	Hal Carlin	Diana Marshall	Jonas Eriksson
Rachel Osborne	Marcel Louis	Lindsey Bateman	David Cauldwell	Alf Montoya	Reuben Cortes
Annabelle Pansin	Ann Xiong	Tara Baldwin	Wendell Guevara	Chase Kendrick	Margaret Yang
Marcie Blanco	Bree Kelley	Jakob Elliott	Antonio Dominguez	Henry Langford	Casey Devine
Jodi Levine	Leo Herbert	Alec Logan	Tamara Hartley	Cliff Butler	Whitney Darden
Eric Goffmann	Terri Drews	Lionel Means	Phil Coley	Jean Costes	Olive Serrano
Laetitia Brown	Helena Rossiter	Celine Pitts	Karen Bevans	Samantha Robbins	Lydia Spencer
Fay Whitman	Jeff Driscoll	Rachel Sosa	Rod Carlton	Deirdre Corbett	Douglas Hanna
Bonita Perez	Carla Pollock	Daisy Prater	Jeremiah Harper	Emma Ferguson	Victor Rodrigues
Sarah Bennett	Annabel Chandler	Brian Easton	Martine Walker	Jan Thayer	Paul Shaver
Trisha Bridges	Beatrice Hezel	Hannah Story	Clelia Walden	Ramon Benavides	Marcus Tyson
Bernadette Fabius	Harry Green	Erica Marks	Walter Delong	Julian Ashley	Leslie Thompson
Linda Segura	Henrietta Mansfield	Shirley Keen	Dan Gould	Larry Tucker	Benita Von Stein
Kerry Thatcher	Gertrude Abbey	RachelWhitney	Sebastian Walton	Keith Farmer	Di Kelley
Melvin Boyce	Gillian Smith	Naomi Buchanan	Malena Read	Mitzi Gor	Dorothy Montgomery
Gordon Roberts	Gail Bradley	Emily Harvey	Alice Wily	Conrad Shields	Martha Watkins
Edwin Gold	Chantal Dupont	Sam Alexander	Mary-Anne Dudley	Jasmine Gifford	Jake Watson
Alexander Keith	Charlie Dart	Bernard Battle	Larry Stubbs	Rachel Shirley	Darryl Williams
Patricia Timmons	Liam Woodiwiss	Toby Gifford	Trena Fields	Louise Blackwell	Piotr Ziniewicz
Lindsey Swift	Lee Brown	Helen Freemantle	Helena Dixon	Wayne Newsome	Miriam Rice-Evans

Happy Together

You are now officially a couple. But what makes your love special, unprecedented, unique? Trace the salient features of your relationship here, from your favourite song to your favourite jokes. Spend some quality time together, just the two of you and your Couple's Book.

Love curve

So you love each other. But how much? Answer that
perennial lover's question with our love curve, where you
can trace your feelings towards each other day by day.
The closer the two curves get, the stronger your love.

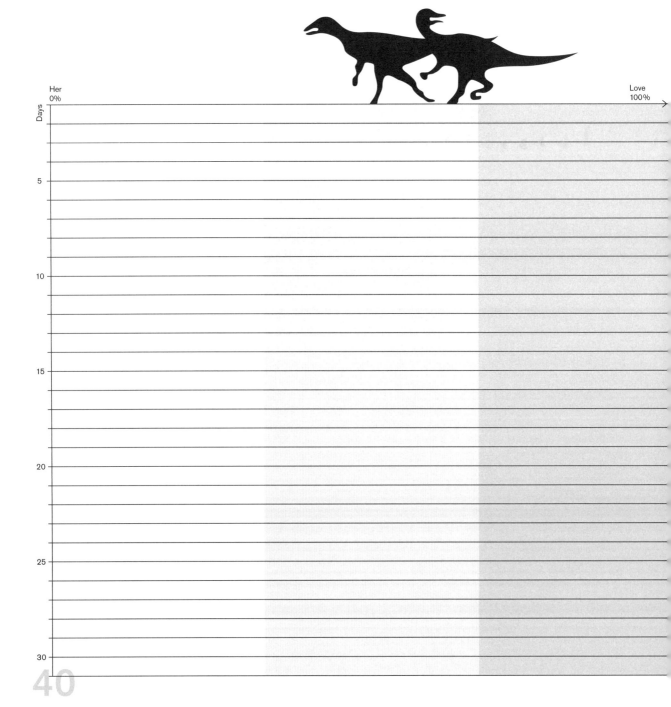

Her
0%

Love
100%

Days

5

10

15

20

25

30

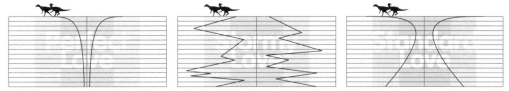

Keep hold of each month's results and you will be able to track your love curve over a lifetime. Here are a few typical examples.

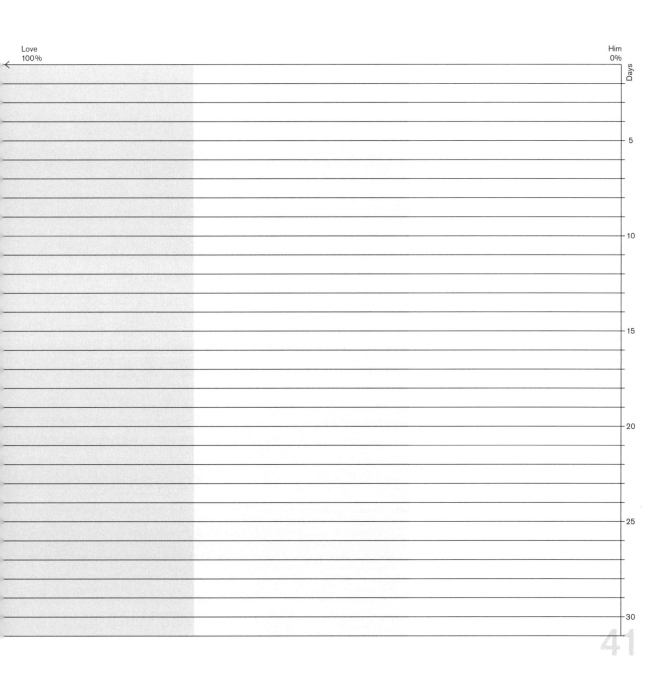

Love
100%

Him
0%

Days

5

10

15

20

25

30

Our favourite things

It shouldn't take long before your couple begins to acquire its own identity, and "I" is replaced by "we". Embrace this merger of your tastes and desires, and list "our" favourites here. They are at the core of your couplehood, so take time to get them right.

Our films	
1	*Casablanca*
2	Elf
3	Romantic Comedy
4	
5	
6	
7	
8	
9	
10	

Our books	
1	*Wuthering Heights*
2	Angels + Demons
3	
4	
5	
6	
7	
8	
9	
10	

Our art	
1	*"The Kiss" by Rodin*
2	Eyes by James Wuyper
3	
4	
5	
6	
7	
8	
9	
10	

Our dreams	
1	Beautiful Home
2	Baby (2 if good)
3	Salon debt free
4	Romantic Vacation 4 eve
5	
6	
7	
8	
9	
10	

Our song

Stevie Wonder *All In Love Is Fair*	☐	Al Green *Let's Stay Together*	☐	Stevie Wonder *I Just Called To Say I Love You*	☐
The Beatles *It's Only Love*	☐	Elvis Presley *Always On My Mind*	☐	Leo Sayer *I Can't Stop Loving You (though I try)*	☐
Elvis Presley *Love Me Tender*	☐	Police *Every Breath You Take*	☐	Ella Fitzgerald *Everytime We Say Goodbye*	☐
The Bee Gees *How Deep Is Your Love*	☐	Bill Withers *Lean On Me*	☐	Billy Joel *I Love You Just The Way You Are*	☐
The Beatles *And I Love Her*	☐	John Paul Young *Love Is In The Air*	☐	Righteous Bros *You've Lost That Lovin' Feelin'*	☐
Sinead O'Connor *Nothing Compares To You*	☐	The Supremes *You Can't Hurry Love*	☐	The Searchers *Sweets For My Sweet*	☐
Chris De Burgh *Lady In Red*	☐	Sonny & Cher *I Got You Babe*	☐	The Shirelles *Will You Still Love Me Tomorrow*	☐
Jennifer Rush *The Power Of Love*	☐	Frank Valli *Can't Take My Eyes Off You*	☐	George Michael *Careless Whisper*	☐
Bryan Adams *Everything I Do I Do It For You*	☐	The Carpenters *Close To You*	☐	Stevie Wonder *You Are The Sunshine Of My Life*	☐
		The Scorpions *Still Loving You*	☐	Tavares *Heaven Must Be Missing An Angel*	☐

Our favourite restaurants	
1	Bonterra
2	Oriental Pheonix
3	Living Room
4	
5	

Our favourite picnic spots	
1	
2	
3	
4	
5	

Our favourite dishes	
1	White + Round
2	Steak + Potatoes
3	
4	
5	

Our favourite ingredients	
1	Love + hot sauce
2	Olives
3	Vodka only grey goose.
4	
5	

Staple favourite restaurant bills here ━━━━━━━ ➤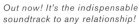

Our favourite recipe

Words of wisdom 2

Søren and Karen love eating together, though they are limited by the lack of restaurants in the Jalberg district. "Cooking together is a thing of recreation and much relaxes," confirms Søren. "The dish, that we make, is frequently Heringsuppé. I fish the herings. She salts them and inserts them in the pot. It is very edible, if you like fish. You can also make it with beef shoulder. But we have not ourselves." Karen adds: "I cook and Søren makes the dishes."

43

Our honeymoon
aaaahhh...

Wild
thing!

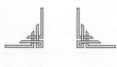

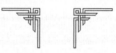

Venice – gotta love
that gondola!

Check out
those haircuts!

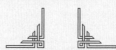

Camera timer
went off early!!!

Working
on that tan...

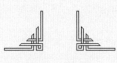

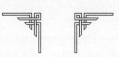

Now we're skiing along,
now we're not!

Waiter "Giorgio" took
this one – molto romantic

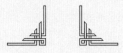

45

Second opinions

At some point you've emerged from your cocoon and introduced each other to your social circle. Friends provide a very welcome corrective to your love-tinted vision. Check with those who know you best whether they think you have chosen a suitable match.

IMP
To confirm you a
photobooth with y

	Her Best Friend
Photo	Name:...
	Best friend since:...........................
	Opinion of the relationship:
	....
	....
	....
	....
	....
	....

	Her Friend 1
Photo	Name:...
	Friend since:.................................
	Opinion of the relationship:
	....
	....
	....
	....
	....
	....

	Her Friend 2
Photo	Name:...
	Friend since:.................................
	Opinion of the relationship:
	....
	....
	....
	....
	....
	....

	Her Friend 3
Photo	Name:...
	Friend since:.................................
	Opinion of the relationship:
	....
	....
	....
	....
	....
	....

	Her Friend 4
Photo	Name:...
	Friend since:.................................
	Opinion of the relationship:
	....
	....
	....
	....
	....
	....

	Her Friend 5
Photo	Name:...
	Friend since:.................................
	Opinion of the relationship:
	....
	....
	....
	....
	....
	....

VETO! We the undersigned friends feel that this relationship is so unsuitable that we have no choice but to veto it. Reason:...

ORTANT!

lose friends, photos *must* be taken in a
and your close friend "goofing around".

Correct

Incorrect

His Best Friend

Name:...
Best friend since:...........................
Opinion of the relationship:
....
....
....
....
....

Photo

His Friend 1

Name:...
Friend since:.....................................
Opinion of the relationship:
....
....
....
....
....

Photo

His Friend 2

Name:...
Friend since:.....................................
Opinion of the relationship:
....
....
....
....
....

Photo

His Friend 3

Name:...
Friend since:.....................................
Opinion of the relationship:
....
....
....
....
....

Photo

His Friend 4

Name:...
Friend since:.....................................
Opinion of the relationship:
....
....
....
....
....

Photo

His Friend 5

Name:...
Friend since:.....................................
Opinion of the relationship:
....
....
....
....
....

Photo

....Signatures:..

Things to do together

The key to long-lasting coupledom is spending quality time together on mutually satisfactory projects, from replanting the garden to trekking across the Himalayas. Here are some fun tasks to keep you busy together. Answers on www.couplesbook.com!

Wordsearch Find the following love-related words: Romantic, Calm, Wonderful, Date, Amour, Intercourse, Cuddle, Love, Ballad, Intimate, Barry White, Shag, Flirting, Touch, Tender, Goat, Couple, Hug, Cute.

R	W	O	N	D	E	R	F	U	L	C	R	R	R
B	O	A	R	R	D	R	R	R	I	U	R	R	
A	R	M	R	R	A	R	T	E	N	D	E	R	
R	R	O	A	R	T	R	I	R	T	D	R	R	
R	R	U	R	N	E	N	R	G	E	L	R	R	
Y	R	R	R	T	R	N	R	R	E	R	R		
W	R	R	R	I	R	I	R	E	C	U	T	E	
H	R	B	M	R	T	R	C	V	O	R	R		
I	R	A	R	R	O	R	C	O	U	P	L	E	
T	T	L	I	R	U	T	R	L	R	H	R	R	
E	R	L	R	R	C	A	L	M	S	U	R	R	
R	F	A	R	R	H	O	R	R	E	G	R	R	
R	R	D	R	R	R	G	S	H	A	G	R	R	

Romantic Riddle...

My first is in love but not in vote
My second is in seduce
        but not in decides
My third is in sex but not in exit
My fourth is in stray but not in play
My whole will consume you!

Solution: __ U S T

Spot the difference There are ten differences between these two pictures. Spot five each!

1

2
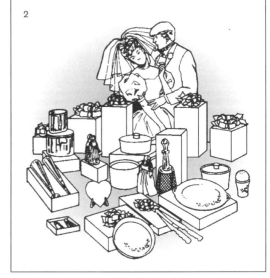

48

Lady labyrinth Will the man find his lover?...

Odd one out Who doesn't belong here???

a   b   c   d
e   f   g   h
i   j   k   l
m   n   o   p

CROSSWORD With the two of you, this should be a piece of cake!

FOOL FOR LOVE	AS HOT AS UR LOVE		I WANT U TO SEE	NOT GOOD IN BED		GOOD LOOK-ING!	KEEPS LOVING WHEELS TURNING	COULD LOOSEN THINGS UP		
KUNG	*i*	HELP ON DATE			SHOULD BE RED			IF LOVE CAN'T BE BOUGHT		
m		PULSATING								
A			LOVE CAN TURN							
			U IN BED							
FELT LITTLE LOVE				WHERE WE MET						
	NOT IDEAL PARTNER FOR USSR			OF A WOM-AN	S C E N T					
TOO COR-RECT							FOR GIRL NOT WOMAN	WHEN I DON'T BEHAVE		
PLACE WHEN U CAN'T FIND		I WANT TO TAKE YOU THERE							WE DON'T LIKE HAVING ONE
WANT TO TAKE YOU TO									
	ROMEO MISS HER								
YOU DRIVE ME									

Love lines Draw two love arrows across the box to leave seven hearts in each part. Use a ruler!

Love-mess! Who will get the hunk?

1   2   3

49

Doodle Together Special

These pages invite you to pick up your crayons and doodle at leisure. This will enhance your relationship and make for a fun evening at any point, but it is particularly recommended when you've had a row and can't bring yourselves to speak (though hate and death-related doodles are prohibited).

Spirals Spirals are indicative of a frustrated mind engaged in a fruitless search for meaning. Doodling spirals together shows that neither of you feel the relationship is going anywhere; they represent a black hole that sucks your emotions in and chews them up. This is not generally considered good.

Crisscross Crisscrossing is doodling at its most wholesome; it speaks of order and purpose. Couples who crisscross together probably enjoy a stable, emotionally mature relationship, where both pull their weight. They have definite plans for their future and their privileged offspring usually goes on to one of the better universities.

Cats Cat doodling is a sign of deep insecurity, associated with jealousy and mistrust. Couples who doodle cats are suspicious of each other, and paradoxically, they are thus more prone to cheating. If the doodled cats are black with oval eyes and long spiky tails, it is highly unlikely the relationship will last more than a few months.

Love hearts Couples who doodle love hearts together lack a fully formed sense of irony. Their relationship is largely based on media-inspired clichés, and their sense of self is dangerously dependent on being part of a couple. Unless something punctures their bubble though, they may go through life blissfully happy.

Compliments

Love needs constant reassurance to keep it alive. Flatter each other with spontaneous compliments from this list. Tick them off as you make them so you don't repeat yourselves. And if there's one you'd particularly like to receive, try circling it discreetly.

You're almost as good looking as me!

Tick ■	Tick ■	Tick ■
You are my sunshine	*You are the light of my life*	*Have I told you how pretty you look*
Tick ■	Tick ■	Tick ■
I am speechless at your beauty	*You're so witty!*	*I love everything about you*
Tick ■	Tick ■	Tick ■
Thank heaven for you	*You look "hot" tonight*	*That hat really suits you*
Tick ■	Tick ■	Tick ■
I must be the luckiest man / woman alive	*You're very special to me*	*Your body is my temple*

Tick ☐	Tick ☐	Tick ☐
I love the way you (insert activity)	*That meal you cooked was delicious*	*You are all woman*
You light my fire	*My! It's huge!*	*You're the love of my life*
I can't get enough of your (insert body part)	*You are sex on legs*	*You smell good (today)*
I feel safe with you	*You so deserve that promotion honey*	*You're my knight in shining armour*
You always make my day	*Life without you ain't worth living*	*I don't just love you, I lurve you*

Our social life

Occasionally you will need to venture together into the outside world, if only to convince acquaintances that your partner is not imaginary. It may not always be appropriate to carry your Couple's Book with you to social events, which is why it's extremely important to pay close attention to these pages now.

The Social Event (use this basic format to keep tabs on your social diaries)

Category of event: Party □ Dinner party □ Bar mitzvah □ Wedding □ Other (specify:..................................)□ Date:.................

Inviter: Friend of hers □ Friend of his □ Her relative □ His relative □ Her colleague □ His colleague □ Other (specify:...............................)□

Is she happy to attend? Yes □ No □ If he insists □ Is he happy to attend? Yes □ No □ If she insists □

RSVP? She will □ He will □ Just turn up □ We're not going and that's final □

Favourite stories about each other	Anecdotes heard too many times	Blatant lies heard too many times
1	1	1 ....
2	2	2 ....
3	3	3 ....
4	4	4 ....
5	5	5 ....

Agreed distress signals at parties

Hand in one's hair   Staring at one's feet   Rubbing one's nose   Looking at one's watch

Alcohol limit before personality changes

Her

Him

Red Card
I demand that we leave this party now as you're getting embarrassingly drunk.

Our couple friends: Invite to couples-only events

	1	2	3
.... &	☐	☐	☐
.... &	☐	☐	☐
.... &	☐	☐	☐
.... &	☐	☐	☐
.... &	☐	☐	☐
.... &	☐	☐	☐
.... &	☐	☐	☐
.... &	☐	☐	☐
.... &	☐	☐	☐
.... &	☐	☐	☐
.... &	☐	☐	☐
.... &	☐	☐	☐

1. Invite to dinner parties

2. Invite to tennis doubles

3. Invite to bridge

Our single friends: Draw arrows to match them up*

Words of wisdom 3

"When we met first, Søren was a shy one," reveals Karen. "He would not speak to many, because on the boat there is none to talk to. So he was not very much practised. But then he started to go out to the maritime bar and drink, and that helped him meet other ones. It was too much help after some few years, because he would fall sleepy drunk in the snow and that was dangerous. But now after the cirrhosis he is controlled and we have many friends. Every month we meet them, at the Jalberg town hall. We speak the gossip with them about the fishwives."

Forward thinking: Friends that would make suitable godparents

....
....
....
....
....
....
....
....

*If couple friends break up, they should be transferred immediately to the single friends category, though take care not to try to match them up with each other by mistake.

Synchronicity

How attuned are you to each other? Find out by spending a day together, then each writing a diary account of it here. Compare the two versions of events and discover if you are both on the same page. NB: no peeking over your partner's shoulder as they write!

Her day

0800
0830
0900
0930
1000
1030
1100
1130
1200
1230
1300
1330
1400
1430
1500
1530
1600
1630
1700
1730
1800
1830
1900
1930
2000
2030
2100
2130
2200
2230
2300
2330
2400

0800..
0830..
0900..
0930..
1000..
1030..
1100..
1130..
1200..
1230..
1300..
1330..
1400..
1430..
1500..
1530..
1600..
1630..
1700..
1730..
1800..
1830..
1900..
1930..
2000..
2030..
2100..
2130..
2200..
2230..
2300..
2330..
2400..

57

Gold stars

Even if you both believe you would do anything for each other, it doesn't hurt to have incentives. Do something thoughtful for your partner, like running them a bubble bath, and win a star (cut it out carefully). When you have accumulated ten stars, you may exchange them for a sexual favour of your choice.

59

Holiday log

When you look back in your old age, you won't remember making cocoa for each other, you'll remember the sunset over the Andes, swimming with dolphins in the Indian Ocean, and climbing Kilimanjaro together. Plan your joint romantic trips on this page, and take your love on tour.

Location	Date	Duration	Method of transport	Romantic highlight	Assessment	Would we return?
					.... /20	Yes ☐ No ☐
					.... /20	Yes ☐ No ☐
					.... /20	Yes ☐ No ☐
					.... /20	Yes ☐ No ☐
					.... /20	Yes ☐ No ☐
					.... /20	Yes ☐ No ☐
					.... /20	Yes ☐ No ☐
					.... /20	Yes ☐ No ☐
					.... /20	Yes ☐ No ☐
					.... /20	Yes ☐ No ☐
					.... /20	Yes ☐ No ☐
					.... /20	Yes ☐ No ☐
					.... /20	Yes ☐ No ☐
					.... /20	Yes ☐ No ☐
					.... /20	Yes ☐ No ☐
					.... /20	Yes ☐ No ☐
					.... /20	Yes ☐ No ☐
					.... /20	Yes ☐ No ☐
					.... /20	Yes ☐ No ☐
					.... /20	Yes ☐ No ☐
					.... /20	Yes ☐ No ☐
					.... /20	Yes ☐ No ☐
					.... /20	Yes ☐ No ☐
					.... /20	Yes ☐ No ☐
					.... /20	Yes ☐ No ☐
					.... /20	Yes ☐ No ☐
					.... /20	Yes ☐ No ☐
					.... /20	Yes ☐ No ☐

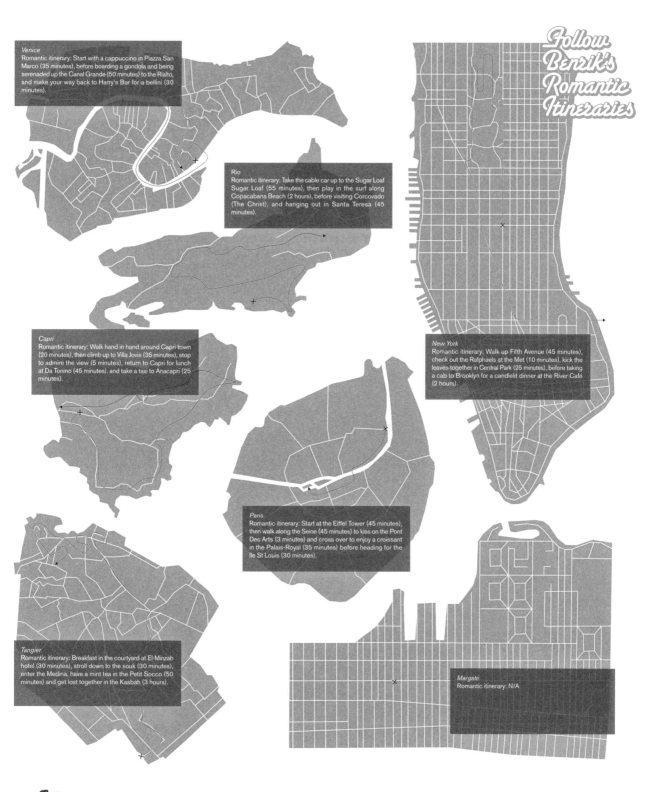

Venice
Romantic itinerary: Start with a cappuccino in Piazza San Marco (35 minutes), before boarding a gondola and being serenaded up the Canal Grande (50 minutes) to the Rialto, and make your way back to Harry's Bar for a bellini (30 minutes).

Rio
Romantic itinerary: Take the cable car up to the Sugar Loaf Sugar Loaf (55 minutes), then play in the surf along Copacabana Beach (2 hours), before visiting Corcovado (The Christ), and hanging out in Santa Teresa (45 minutes).

Capri
Romantic itinerary: Walk hand in hand around Capri town (20 minutes), then climb up to Villa Jovis (35 minutes), stop to admire the view (5 minutes), return to Capri for lunch at Da Tonino (45 minutes), and take a taxi to Anacapri (25 minutes).

New York
Romantic itinerary: Walk up Fifth Avenue (45 minutes), check out the Rafphaels at the Met (10 minutes), kick the leaves together in Central Park (25 minutes), before taking a cab to Brooklyn for a candlelit dinner at the River Café (2 hours).

Paris
Romantic itinerary: Start at the Eiffel Tower (45 minutes), then walk along the Seine (45 minutes) to kiss on the Pont Des Arts (3 minutes) and cross over to enjoy a croissant in the Palais-Royal (35 minutes) before heading for the Ile St Louis (30 minutes).

Tangier
Romantic itinerary: Breakfast in the courtyard at El-Minzah hotel (30 minutes), stroll down to the souk (30 minutes), enter the Medina, have a mint tea in the Petit Socco (50 minutes) and get lost together in the Kasbah (3 hours).

Margate
Romantic itinerary: N/A

Taking the Couple's Book with you: The Couple's Book is not primarily designed to travel, but follow these precautions and you should be safe. A) Keep it away from direct sunlight. B) Do not let it out of your sight. Most insurance policies will only reimburse the cover price, not the emotional value. Keep it in the hotel safe, or under your pillow, as you would at home. C) Report any theft to the local authorities. Useful phrases: ¡Se ha robado nuestro Couple's Book! On a volé notre Couple's Book! Unser Couple's Book ist gestohlen worden!

Time alone

Trust the cliché, you need your space. If you don't spend some time apart, you'll end up that way. That is why we provide each of you with your very own page, which you should use to plan and lead your separate lives.

Her page (private space)	*No peeking*

....
....
....
....
....
....
....
....
....
....
....
....
....
....
....
....
....
....
....
....
....
....
....
....
....
....
....

Things I like to do that he doesn't...

Friends I like to see that he doesn't..

TV I like to watch that he doesn't..

Music I like to listen to that he doesn't...

How much time should you spend alone?					
First month: 2 minutes a day	Second month: 5 minutes a day	Months 3 to 12: 15 minutes a day	Years 2 to 5: 1 hour a day	Years 5 to 10: 2 hours a day	Years 10+: by now, you can be alone together

His page (private space)   *No peeking*

....
....
....
....
....
....
....
....
....
....
....
....
....
....
....
....
....
....
....
....
....
....
....

Things I like to do that she doesn't...

Friends I like to see that she doesn't..

TV I like to watch that she doesn't...

Music I like to listen to that she doesn't...

Visitors' Book

Your love should be like a ray of sunshine, brightening up everyone's day. Allow everybody who visits you to thank you in this well-presented visitors' section, where they may comment on what a lovely couple you make.

Visitor(s): _Mikey_	From: _Speedi Pizza_	Date: ...02.../...11.../...04...	Would you ever visit this couple again? Yes ☐ No ■ Maybe ☐
Comments on the couple: _Errr... Thanks 4 the tipp. Hope you like your pizza_ _(sorry again I forgot your bevrages)_			
Visitor(s):	From:	Date: ..../.............../...............	Would you ever visit this couple again? Yes ☐ No ☐ Maybe ☐
Comments on the couple:			
Visitor(s):	From:	Date: ..../.............../...............	Would you ever visit this couple again? Yes ☐ No ☐ Maybe ☐
Comments on the couple:			
Visitor(s):	From:	Date: ..../.............../...............	Would you ever visit this couple again? Yes ☐ No ☐ Maybe ☐
Comments on the couple:			
Visitor(s):	From:	Date: ..../.............../...............	Would you ever visit this couple again? Yes ☐ No ☐ Maybe ☐
Comments on the couple:			
Visitor(s):	From:	Date: ..../.............../...............	Would you ever visit this couple again? Yes ☐ No ☐ Maybe ☐
Comments on the couple:			
Visitor(s):	From:	Date: ..../.............../...............	Would you ever visit this couple again? Yes ☐ No ☐ Maybe ☐
Comments on the couple:			
Visitor(s):	From:	Date: ..../.............../...............	Would you ever visit this couple again? Yes ☐ No ☐ Maybe ☐
Comments on the couple:			
Visitor(s):	From:	Date: ..../.............../...............	Would you ever visit this couple again? Yes ☐ No ☐ Maybe ☐
Comments on the couple:			

Visitor(s):	From:	Date: .... / .... /	Would you ever visit this couple again? Yes ☐ No ☐ Maybe ☐
Comments on the couple:			

Visitor(s):	From:	Date: .... / .... /	Would you ever visit this couple again? Yes ☐ No ☐ Maybe ☐
Comments on the couple:			

Visitor(s):	From:	Date: .... / .... /	Would you ever visit this couple again? Yes ☐ No ☐ Maybe ☐
Comments on the couple:			

Visitor(s):	From:	Date: .... / .... /	Would you ever visit this couple again? Yes ☐ No ☐ Maybe ☐
Comments on the couple:			

Visitor(s):	From:	Date: .... / .... /	Would you ever visit this couple again? Yes ☐ No ☐ Maybe ☐
Comments on the couple:			

Visitor(s):	From:	Date: .... / .... /	Would you ever visit this couple again? Yes ☐ No ☐ Maybe ☐
Comments on the couple:			

Visitor(s):	From:	Date: .... / .... /	Would you ever visit this couple again? Yes ☐ No ☐ Maybe ☐
Comments on the couple:			

Visitor(s):	From:	Date: .... / .... /	Would you ever visit this couple again? Yes ☐ No ☐ Maybe ☐
Comments on the couple:			

Visitor(s):	From:	Date: .... / .... /	Would you ever visit this couple again? Yes ☐ No ☐ Maybe ☐
Comments on the couple:			

Visitor(s):	From:	Date: .... / .... /	Would you ever visit this couple again? Yes ☐ No ☐ Maybe ☐
Comments on the couple:			

Visitor(s):	From:	Date: .... / .... /	Would you ever visit this couple again? Yes ☐ No ☐ Maybe ☐
Comments on the couple:			

Visitor(s):	From:	Date: .... / .... /	Would you ever visit this couple again? Yes ☐ No ☐ Maybe ☐
Comments on the couple:			

Celebrity couples

These pages are devoted to the celebrity couples amongst you, in recognition of the special pressures placed on your love. May the golden handcuffs of fame not impede your happiness, though if they do, there's always the money.

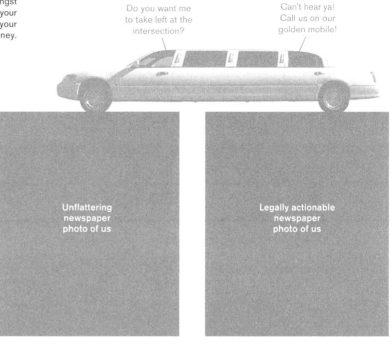

Do you want me to take left at the intersection?

Can't hear ya! Call us on our golden mobile!

Favourite newspaper photo of us	Unflattering newspaper photo of us	Legally actionable newspaper photo of us

Our favourite journalists	Our favourite fans	Our favourite stalkers
1	1	1 ....
2	2	2 ....
3	3	3 ....
4	4	4 ....
5	5	5 ....

Internet sites about us

www..
www..
www..
www..
www..
www..
www..
www..
www..
Our blue movie is available on www..
....

Leaked by gardener ☐ plumber ☐ assistant ☐ cable guy ☐

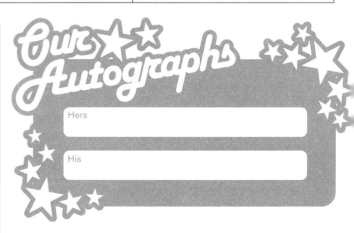

Our Autographs

Hers

His

Do not leave your Celebrity Couple's Book lying around near journalists, unless you are deliberately trying to get into the papers.
☐ We are deliberately trying to get into the papers. The juicy pages are:............
☐ We are not trying to get into the papers and have genuinely mislaid this book.

Our love

What she loves most about him... What he loves most about her..

What she loves most about herself..

....

....

....

What he loves most about himself...

....

....

....

Intentions

☐ We are in this for the long-term, and are prepared to ignore blatant media violations of our privacy, speciously justified by reference to the so-called "public interest".

☐ We are in this for a short sharp boost to our flagging careers, and recognize that it will end when we exhaust each other's gnat-like attention spans.

Celebrity + Nobody matches

Warning: the celebrity/nobody couple stands even less chance of success than the double celebrity one. At best, the nobody will become a celebrity by association and will develop celebrity vices. At worst, they will be laughed at for being a nobody until the celebrity tires of them and casts them back into nobody-land, where they will attempt to conjure up a minor cable TV presenting job out of their very public humiliation. Don't go there.

REMINDER!

Honey don't forget I'm on TV tonight! Watch me at:

....(time)

on:..(channel)

Confidentiality Agreement

Benrik

We solemnly swear never to divulge the secrets of this our Couple's Book to anyone, unless some magazine pays a minimum of .... for it.
Witnessed by:

Her manager...

His manager...

Her agent..

His agent..

Her trainer..

His trainer...

Her physio...

His physio...

Her dietitian..

His dietitian..

Celebrity couples in history

Antony and Cleopatra
Antony and Cleopatra both pursued very high-powered careers in competitive fields. But they were unable to reconcile their lifestyles and spend enough quality time on life projects together, so they both committed suicide. Unhappy ending.

Romeo and Juliet
Romeo and Juliet were initially infatuated but sadly came from insufficiently similar backgrounds, a frequent cause of relationship failure. Lack of proper long-term compatibility meant they both had to die horribly. Unhappy ending.

Napoleon and Josephine
Josephine was 6 years older than Napoleon, which created an age gap issue. In addition, Napoleon travelled a lot on business for long periods of time, which led to marital tension and infidelity. They divorced. Unhappy ending.

Bonnie and Clyde
Bonnie and Clyde were compatible in terms of lifestyle preferences, but failed to lay the groundwork for an enduring long-term relationship, for instance by setting up joint financial planning for retirement. They were shot. Unhappy ending.

Pillow Talk

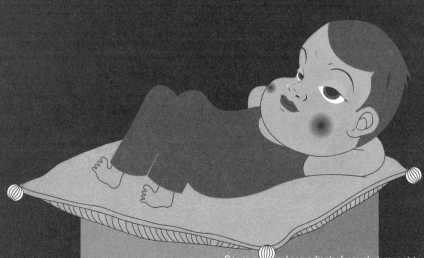

Sex is a critical ingredient of coupledom, not to mention one of the more pleasant biological imperatives. No matter how unsuited you seem, if you get it right in bed, you stand a good chance of lasting. Document and improve your lust life between these sheets.

Our Naked

She draws him

Example:

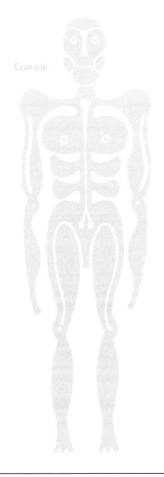

Bodies

Draw your naked partner as faithfully and lovingly as you can. Think of their body as the temple at which you worship. Caution: do not attempt this drunk, do not attempt it during sex, and, above all, do not take poor draughtsmanship as a personal insult. Circle your 3 favourite bits of each other in red, and lavish particular care on them next time you make love.

He draws her

Example:

71

Our fantasies

Sex is in the mind, as every schoolboy knows. Now that you've drawn each other's bodies, explore each other's desires. The sexual imagination is a dark and notoriously unfathomable beast. But try fathoming it a bit here, and you will both be rewarded.

Fantasies		
Author:............................ Title:............................... Basic plot:....................... .... Partner's response: O-K! □ Not my cup of tea □ I'm outta here □	Author:............................ Title:............................... Basic plot:....................... .... Partner's response: O-K! □ Not my cup of tea □ I'm outta here □	Author:............................ Title:............................... Basic plot:....................... .... Partner's response: O-K! □ Not my cup of tea □ I'm outta here □
Author:............................ Title:............................... Basic plot:....................... .... Partner's response: O-K! □ Not my cup of tea □ I'm outta here □	Author:............................ Title:............................... Basic plot:....................... .... Partner's response: O-K! □ Not my cup of tea □ I'm outta here □	Author:............................ Title:............................... Basic plot:....................... .... Partner's response: O-K! □ Not my cup of tea □ I'm outta here □
Author:............................ Title:............................... Basic plot:....................... .... Partner's response: O-K! □ Not my cup of tea □ I'm outta here □	Author:............................ Title:............................... Basic plot:....................... .... Partner's response: O-K! □ Not my cup of tea □ I'm outta here □	Author:............................ Title:............................... Basic plot:....................... .... Partner's response: O-K! □ Not my cup of tea □ I'm outta here □

Possible ingredients to jog your imagination						
Blindfold	Massage oil	Root vegetables	Marigolds	Farmhouse	Waterbed	Football team
Handcuffs	Whip	Nunnery	Milkmaid	Banana	Frilly knickers	Vibrator
Desert island	Nurse outfit	Tropical storm	Candle	Mail-order dildo	Chastity belt	Haystack
Whipped cream	Pizza delivery	Convertible	School uniforms	Plumber	Best friend	Doberman

Where do her fantasies mostly come from? Mills & Boon □ Cosmo □ Pornography □ Childhood trauma □ Don't know □

Where do his fantasies mostly come from? Pornography □ Porn mags □ Porn videos □ Childhood trauma □ Don't know □

Condensed Kamasutra: Tick every position as you try it.

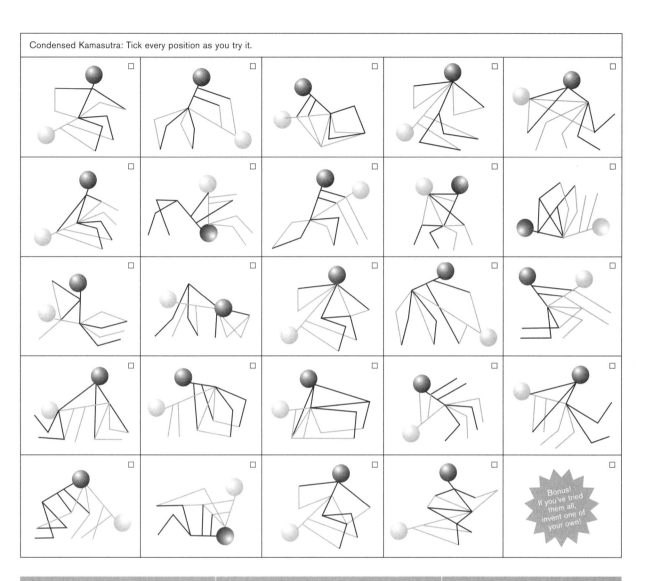

Naughty words
Circle words that turn you on
Cross out words that turn you off

Cock Dick Penis Fanny Rumpy-pumpy
Penetrate Prick Intercourse Come Stop
Orgasm Giddy-up Horny Panties Sex
Suck Donkey Moist Titties Hard Beast
Virgin Rough Dirty Manhood Bad Illegal

Naughty languages
Circle languages that turn you on
Cross out languages that turn you off

Italian French Russian Albanian Spanish
Arabic German Polish Chinese Dutch
Swedish Icelandic Swahili Esperanto
Basque Portuguese Lithuanian Japanese
Finnish Turkish Czech Romanian Yiddish

Pillow talking
Record any particularly memorable or
effective phrases you come up with during
sex so as to use them again.

....
....
....
....
....
....
....
....

Caution: take your book to bed with you by all
means, but store it under the pillow for safe
keeping during intercourse.

Special "shy couples" feature!
Point to where you like to be touched

Our sex counter

Every time you make love is sacred. Don't let a single one of your couplings be forgotten: keep track of these little snatches of heaven by writing each date in one of the boxes. At the end of your life together, you'll be able to look back at your lovemaking tally.

▨ = Dirty weekends

A grid of boxes, each reading "Date......./......./......."

Date / /	Date / /	Date / /	Date / /	Date / /	Date / /	Date / /	Date / /	Date / /	Date / /	Date / /
Date / /	Date / /	Date / /	Date / /	Date / /	Date / /	Date / /	Date / /	Date / /	Date / /	Date / /
Date / /	Date / /	Date / /	Date / /	Date / /	Date / /	Date / /	Date / /	Date / /	Date / /	Date / /
Date / /	Date / /	Date / /	Date / /	Date / /	Date / /	Date / /	Date / /	Date / /	Date / /	Date / /
Date / /	Date / /	Date / /	Date / /	Date / /	Date / /	Date / /	Date / /	Date / /	Date / /	Date / /
Date / /	Date / /	Date / /	Date / /	Date / /	Date / /	Date / /	Date / /	Date / /	Date / /	Date / /
Date / /	Date / /	Date / /	Date / /	Date / /	Date / /	Date / /	Date / /	Date / /	Date / /	Date / /
Date / /	Date / /	Date / /	Date / /	Date / /	Date / /	Date / /	Date / /	Date / /	Date / /	Date / /
Date / /	Date / /	Date / /	Date / /	Date / /	Date / /	Date / /	Date / /	Date / /	Date / /	Date / /
Date / /	Date / /	Date / /	Date / /	Date / /	Date / /	Date / /	Date / /	Date / /	Date / /	Date / /
Date / /	Date / /	Date / /	Date / /	Date / /	Date / /	Date / /	Date / /	Date / /	Date / /	Date / /
Date / /	Date / /	Date / /	Date / /	Date / /	Date / /	Date / /	Date / /	Date / /	Date / /	Date / /
Date / /	Date / /	Date / /	Date / /	Date / /	Date / /	Date / /	Date / /	Date / /	Date / /	Date / /
Date / /	Date / /	Date / /	Date / /	Date / /	Date / /	Date / /	Date / /	Date / /	Date / /	Date / /
Date / /	Date / /	Date / /	Date / /	Date / /	Date / /	Date / /	Date / /	Date / /	Date / /	Date / /
Date / /	Date / /	Date / /	Date / /	Date / /	Date / /	Date / /	Date / /	Date / /	Date / /	Date / /
Date / /	Date / /	Date / /	Date / /	Date / /	Date / /	Date / /	Date / /	Date / /	Date / /	Date / /
Date / /	Date / /	Date / /	Date / /	Date / /	Date / /	Date / /	Date / /	Date / /	Date / /	Date / /
Date / /	Date / /	Date / /	Date / /	Date / /	Date / /	Date / /	Date / /	Date / /	Date / /	Date / /
Date / /	Date / /	Date / /	Date / /	Date / /	Date / /	Date / /	Date / /	Date / /	Date / /	Date / /
Date / /	Date / /	Date / /	Date / /	Date / /	Date / /	Date / /	Date / /	Date / /	Date / /	Date / /
Date / /	Date / /	Date / /	Date / /	Date / /	Date / /	Date / /	Date / /	Date / /	Date / /	Date / /
Date / /	Date / /	Date / /	Date / /	Date / /	Date / /	Date / /	Date / /	Date / /	Date / /	Date / /
Date / /	Date / /	Date / /	Date / /	Date / /	Date / /	Date / /	Date / /	Date / /	Date / /	Date / /
Date / /	Date / /	Date / /	Date / /	Date / /	Date / /	Date / /	Date / /	Date / /	Date / /	Date / /
Date / /	Date / /	Date / /	Date / /	Date / /	Date / /	Date / /	Date / /	Date / /	Date / /	Date / /
Date / /	Date / /	Date / /	Date / /	Date / /	Date / /	Date / /	Date / /	Date / /	Date / /	Date / /
Date / /	Date / /	Date / /	Date / /	Date / /	Date / /	Date / /	Date / /	Date / /	Date / /	Date / /
Date / /	Date / /	Date / /	Date / /	Date / /	Date / /	Date / /	Date / /	Date / /	Date / /	Date / /
Date / /	Date / /	Date / /	Date / /	Date / /	Date / /	Date / /	Date / /	Date / /	Date / /	Date / /
Date / /	Date / /	Date / /	Date / /	Date / /	Date / /	Date / /	Date / /	Date / /	Date / /	Date / /
Date / /	Date / /	Date / /	Date / /	Date / /	Date / /	Date / /	Date / /	Date / /	Date / /	Date / /
Date / /	Date / /	Date / /	Date / /	Date / /	Date / /	Date / /	Date / /	Date / /	Date / /	Date / /
Date / /	Date / /	Date / /	Date / /	Date / /	Date / /	Date / /	Date / /	Date / /	Date / /	Date / /
Date / /	Date / /	Date / /	Date / /	Date / /	Date / /	Date / /	Date / /	Date / /	Date / /	Date / /
Date / /	Date / /	Date / /	Date / /	Date / /	Date / /	Date / /	Date / /	Date / /	Date / /	Date / /
Date / /	Date / /	Date / /	Date / /	Date / /	Date / /	Date / /	Date / /	Date / /	Date / /	Date / /
Date / /	Date / /	Date / /	Date / /	Date / /	Date / /	Date / /	Date / /	Date / /	Date / /	Date / /
Date / /	Date / /	Date / /	Date / /	Date / /	Date / /	Date / /	Date / /	Date / /	Date / /	Date / /
Date / /	Date / /	Date / /	Date / /	Date / /	Date / /	Date / /	Date / /	Date / /	Date / /	Date / /

Vintage orgasms

If you use the Couple's Book on a regular basis, you are bound to enjoy mind-blowing sex. Rejoice in your libido by recording the details of your best orgasms, marking them out of 10. NB: only mutual unfaked orgasms count.

Time..

Duration..

Place...

Position..

.... /10

Time..

Duration..

Place...

Position..

.... /10

Time..

Duration..

Place...

Position..

.... /10

Time..

Duration..

Place...

Position..

.... /10

Time..

Duration..

Place...

Position..

.... /10

Time..

Duration..

Place...

Position..

.... /10

Time..
....
Duration..
....
Place...
....
....
Position...
....
....
.... /10

Time..
....
Duration..
....
Place...
....
....
Position...
....
....
.... /10

Time..
....
Duration..
....
Place...
....
....
Position...
....
....
.... /10

Time..
....
Duration..
....
Place...
....
....
Position...
....
....
.... /10

Time..
....
Duration..
....
Place...
....
....
Position...
....
....
.... /10

Time..
....
Duration..
....
Place...
....
....
Position...
....
....
.... /10

Time..
....
Duration..
....
Place...
....
....
Position...
....
....
.... /10

Time..
....
Duration..
....
Place...
....
....
Position...
....
....
.... /10

Time..
....
Duration..
....
Place...
....
....
Position...
....
....
.... /10

Our naughtiest sex act

Some sexual matters are beyond words. Spare your blushes by drawing the filthiest thing the two of you have done. It doesn't have to be anatomically correct, just as long as you don't invent any extra limbs. Don't forget to include location, facial expressions, and any bystanders.

Just whose idea was this? Her ◼ Him ◼ Does it still seem like a good idea now? Her ◼ Him ◼ Would you do it again? Her ◼ Him ◼

Our blue movie

With the advent of digital technology, anyone can write, film and star in their own perfectly competent blue movie for next to nothing. And if you're pleased with the result, why not hawk it to the adult movie industry? If love can move mountains, surely it can help with the rent. Use this storyboard to plan your script.

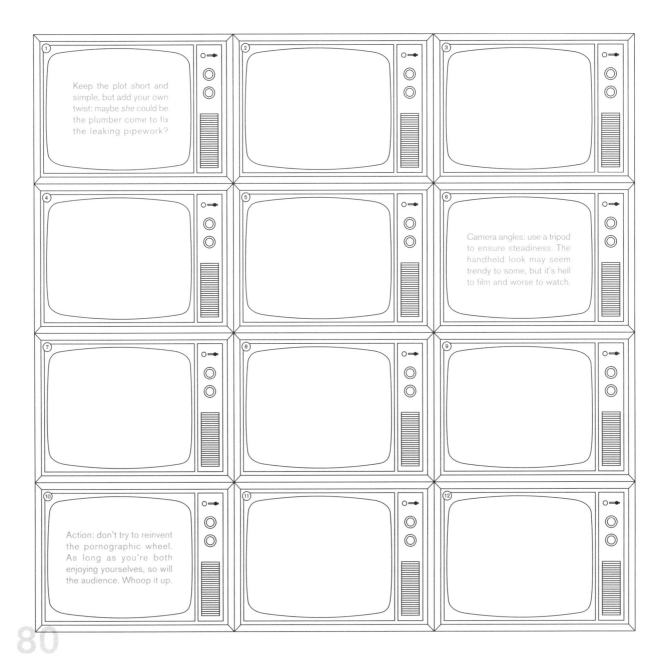

Keep the plot short and simple, but add your own twist: maybe *she* could be the plumber come to fix the leaking pipework?

Camera angles: use a tripod to ensure steadiness. The handheld look may seem trendy to some, but it's hell to film and worse to watch.

Action: don't try to reinvent the pornographic wheel. As long as you're both enjoying yourselves, so will the audience. Whoop it up.

14. Dialogue: the less the better, otherwise it gets tricky to dub into German. Also try to keep it single-minded, you can discuss the shopping later.

19. Soundtrack: refrain from adding on your very favourite Barry White love tracks, as this is a violation of copyright and could lead to a costly and embarrassing lawsuit.

24. Ending: simply fade away gently after the money shot. Crediting yourselves as directors, writers, actors, editors, stuntmen and so on will not add to the film's erotic charge. Good luck!

81

Problem page

Even the most libidinous of couples will eventually face a sexual hiccup. You should raise this in the logbook first, but you can go into greater detail here. And remember: it is nothing to be ashamed of, although do double-check with each other before showing these pages to mutual friends.

Dry patches: Acceptable excuses include illness, advanced pregnancy, parenthood. "Headache" is such a cliché it can no longer be used, even if true.

Start date...
Finish date..
Total days without sex...............................
Official excuse...
....

Start date...
Finish date..
Total days without sex...............................
Official excuse...
....

Start date...
Finish date..
Total days without sex...............................
Official excuse...
....

Wet patches: Unauthorized fantasies involving other people.

Who...
Real person ☐ Imaginary ☐ Hollywood star ☐
What..
....
When...
Where..

Who...
Real person ☐ Imaginary ☐ Hollywood star ☐
What..
....
When...
Where..

Who...
Real person ☐ Imaginary ☐ Hollywood star ☐
What..
....
When...
Where..

Female problems: Inability to reach orgasm.

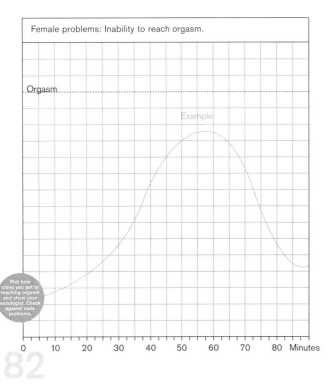

Male problems: Mechanical issues.

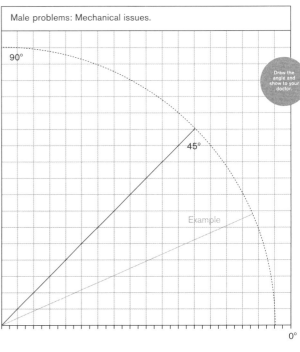

Parents	Grandparents	Greatgrandparents
Mathematical problem	Important historical dates	Shopping list
Ex	Chess	Hiroshima
Offal	The Pope	Castration anxiety

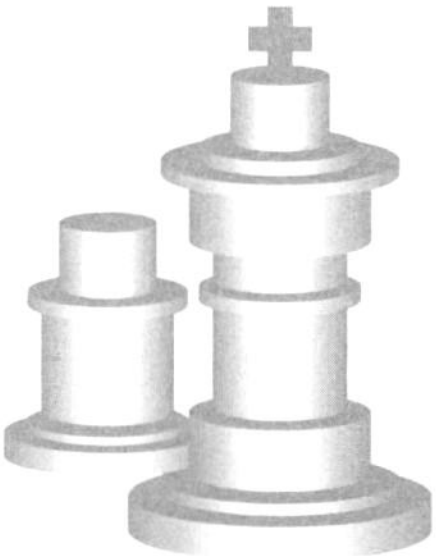

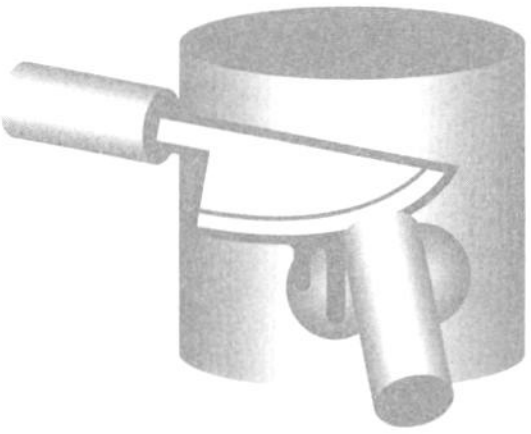

Premature ejaculation: Focus on the following during intercourse and rank in order of delaying effectiveness.

Mathematical problem:

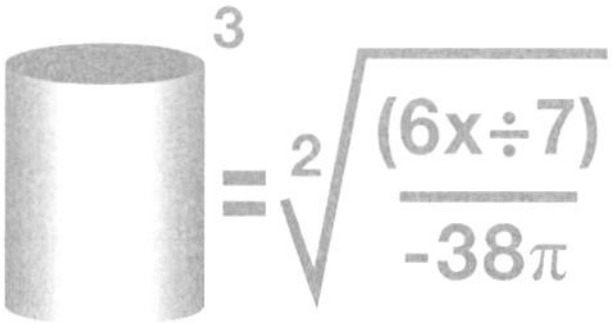

$$\prod{}^3 = \sqrt[2]{\dfrac{(6x \div 7)}{-38\pi}}$$

Shopping list:

EGG
MILK
SAUS
AGE

Logbook

The logbook is the workhorse of the Couple's Book, where you share small problems in order to stop them growing into big expensive divorce lawsuits. You could hire a therapist to do the job, but the logbook might prove less time-consuming, not to mention cheaper.

How to use the logbook

Write the date and the time. Each of you must consult the logbook daily for new comments your partner may have, and reply within 24 hours. Do not let issues fester!

Explain the issue neatly and concisely. If you can't fit it into the two allocated lines, it's probably because you haven't fully thought it through. Try again! You can do it!

Which main category does your comment fall under? Refer to the user-friendly key in the bottom corner of this page, and draw the relevant icon in the category column.

Rank the issue in importance. Fill in one circle for a tiny issue, two for a small one, three for a serious issue, four for a huge problem, and five for a relationship-breaker.

Don't forget! You can also use the logbook for impromptu compliments! If you're not very imaginative on the flattery front, why not simply consult the Compliments page?

There's no reason to be rude like this nasty person! Gratuitous insults get you nowhere. Constructive criticism is what you should offer – and expect to receive!

Category Key	
♡	Emotional
$	Financial
⌂	Domestic
✕	Sexual
＋	Medical
◯	General

Date & Time	Subject	Category	Importance
27/12/04 08:28	*IF THE SINK IS STILL FULL TONIGHT, I'M GETTING A DIVORCE!*	⌂	●●●●●
05/03/03 11:51	*Forgot to tell you, but you looked gorgeous last night.* *If I didn't know you already I'd have chatted you up!*	✕	●●○○○
19/09/92 16:53	*I can't afford this holiday in Paris! Can't we go somewhere local?*	$	●●●○○
11/06/02 23:59	*I'm feeling really tired from work at the moment babe,* *sorry if we've not had much you-know-what*	✕	●●●○○
01/01/05 07:46	*Honey, the milk goes in before the tea*	○	●●●●○
31/03/75 14:40	*You smell good! Is that a new aftershave?*	○	●●○○○
16/08/95 18:03	*I have a confession to make: I've just been to my gynaecologist and she says it is* *thrush after all. Sorry! PS I've left the antibiotics on your desk. No hard feelings?*	+	●○○○○
24/09/07 01:41	*It's 2 in the morning and you're not home. Are you having an affair?*	♡	●●●●●
30/03/88 12:01	*Have you seen my walkman anywhere?*	○	●○○○○
21/02/01 22:49	*For future reference, my G-spot is not within reach of your little toe!*	+	●●●●○
02/07/00 16:10	*Sweetest, if you play that CD once more, I will implode.*	⌂	●●●○○
16/07/04 04:31	*In my dream you were with another woman. I'm going* *home to my mother's to think it through.*	♡	●●●●●
10/12/99 09:14	*Btw I forgot to take the pill and now I'm pregnant. See you tonight!!*	+	●●○○○
03/11/03 18:25	*Thanks for those flowers Rob! You're such a sweetheart!*	♡	●●●●○
03/11/03 18:26	*I'm not Rob, I'm Brian!*	○	●●○○○
25/02/05 02:10	*Hi I'm your burglar tonight. Me and the wife got this book, it's funnee. Gotta rush.*	⌂	●●●●○
14/02/05 00:00:00!	*I HATE YOU! I HATE YOU! YOU'VE RUINED MY LIFE YOU* *BASTARD YOU HORRIBLE PIECE OF SHIT! DIE!!!*	♡	●●●○○
01/01/05 11:45	*Darling, will you marry me?*	♡	●●●●●

Date & Time	Subject	Category	Importance
MARCH 1 8pm	Hi BaBE I LoVE YOU XOXOXOX OXOXOXOXO XOXOXO XO XOXO XOXO	♡	○○○○◉
MARCH 15 4:30	Hi BABE WHAT HAPPENED to our Book? miss you		○○○○○
MARCH 24 4:00	IT MAKES me Sad to NOT HAVE Anything From you Here	♡	◉◉○○○
April 11 8:30pm	I Really don't Like how everything is going. I Am going to Try HARDER	○	◉◉◉◉◉
			○○○○○
			○○○○○
			○○○○○
			○○○○○
			○○○○○
			○○○○○
			○○○○○
			○○○○○
			○○○○○
			○○○○○
			○○○○○
			○○○○○
			○○○○○

Date & Time	Subject	Category	Importance
			○ ○ ○ ○ ○
			○ ○ ○ ○ ○
			○ ○ ○ ○ ○
			○ ○ ○ ○ ○
			○ ○ ○ ○ ○
			○ ○ ○ ○ ○
			○ ○ ○ ○ ○
			○ ○ ○ ○ ○
			○ ○ ○ ○ ○
			○ ○ ○ ○ ○
			○ ○ ○ ○ ○
			○ ○ ○ ○ ○
			○ ○ ○ ○ ○
			○ ○ ○ ○ ○
			○ ○ ○ ○ ○
			○ ○ ○ ○ ○
			○ ○ ○ ○ ○
			○ ○ ○ ○ ○

LUV IS A
4-LETTER
WORD

Date & Time	Subject	Category	Importance
			○ ○ ○ ○ ○
			○ ○ ○ ○ ○
			○ ○ ○ ○ ○
			○ ○ ○ ○ ○
			○ ○ ○ ○ ○
			○ ○ ○ ○ ○
			○ ○ ○ ○ ○
			○ ○ ○ ○ ○
			○ ○ ○ ○ ○
			○ ○ ○ ○ ○
			○ ○ ○ ○ ○
			○ ○ ○ ○ ○
			○ ○ ○ ○ ○
			○ ○ ○ ○ ○
			○ ○ ○ ○ ○
			○ ○ ○ ○ ○
			○ ○ ○ ○ ○
			○ ○ ○ ○ ○

Date & Time	Subject	Category	Importance
			○ ○ ○ ○ ○
			○ ○ ○ ○ ○
			○ ○ ○ ○ ○
			○ ○ ○ ○ ○
			○ ○ ○ ○ ○
			○ ○ ○ ○ ○
			○ ○ ○ ○ ○
			○ ○ ○ ○ ○
			○ ○ ○ ○ ○
			○ ○ ○ ○ ○
			○ ○ ○ ○ ○
			○ ○ ○ ○ ○
			○ ○ ○ ○ ○
			○ ○ ○ ○ ○
			○ ○ ○ ○ ○
			○ ○ ○ ○ ○
			○ ○ ○ ○ ○

Date & Time	Subject	Category	Importance
			○ ○ ○ ○ ○
			○ ○ ○ ○ ○
			○ ○ ○ ○ ○
			○ ○ ○ ○ ○
			○ ○ ○ ○ ○
			○ ○ ○ ○ ○
			○ ○ ○ ○ ○
			○ ○ ○ ○ ○
			○ ○ ○ ○ ○
			○ ○ ○ ○ ○
			○ ○ ○ ○ ○
			○ ○ ○ ○ ○
			○ ○ ○ ○ ○
			○ ○ ○ ○ ○
			○ ○ ○ ○ ○
			○ ○ ○ ○ ○
			○ ○ ○ ○ ○
			○ ○ ○ ○ ○

Date & Time	Subject	Category	Importance
			○ ○ ○ ○ ○
			○ ○ ○ ○ ○
			○ ○ ○ ○ ○
			○ ○ ○ ○ ○
			○ ○ ○ ○ ○
			○ ○ ○ ○ ○
			○ ○ ○ ○ ○
			○ ○ ○ ○ ○
			○ ○ ○ ○ ○
			○ ○ ○ ○ ○
			○ ○ ○ ○ ○
			○ ○ ○ ○ ○
			○ ○ ○ ○ ○
			○ ○ ○ ○ ○
			○ ○ ○ ○ ○
			○ ○ ○ ○ ○
			○ ○ ○ ○ ○
			○ ○ ○ ○ ○

IF LOVE IS A DRUG, GIMME A PRESCRIPTION!

Date & Time	Subject	Category	Importance
			○ ○ ○ ○ ○
			○ ○ ○ ○ ○
			○ ○ ○ ○ ○
			○ ○ ○ ○ ○
			○ ○ ○ ○ ○
			○ ○ ○ ○ ○
			○ ○ ○ ○ ○
			○ ○ ○ ○ ○
			○ ○ ○ ○ ○
			○ ○ ○ ○ ○
			○ ○ ○ ○ ○
			○ ○ ○ ○ ○
			○ ○ ○ ○ ○
			○ ○ ○ ○ ○
			○ ○ ○ ○ ○
			○ ○ ○ ○ ○
			○ ○ ○ ○ ○
			○ ○ ○ ○ ○

I AM DRUNK ON
YOUR LOVE!
BURP!

Date & Time	Subject	Category	Importance
			○ ○ ○ ○ ○
			○ ○ ○ ○ ○
			○ ○ ○ ○ ○
			○ ○ ○ ○ ○
			○ ○ ○ ○ ○
			○ ○ ○ ○ ○
			○ ○ ○ ○ ○
			○ ○ ○ ○ ○
			○ ○ ○ ○ ○
			○ ○ ○ ○ ○
			○ ○ ○ ○ ○
			○ ○ ○ ○ ○
			○ ○ ○ ○ ○
			○ ○ ○ ○ ○
			○ ○ ○ ○ ○
			○ ○ ○ ○ ○
			○ ○ ○ ○ ○
			○ ○ ○ ○ ○

Date & Time	Subject	Category	Importance
			$\circ\circ\circ\circ\circ$
			$\circ\circ\circ\circ\circ$
			$\circ\circ\circ\circ\circ$
			$\circ\circ\circ\circ\circ$
			$\circ\circ\circ\circ\circ$
			$\circ\circ\circ\circ\circ$
			$\circ\circ\circ\circ\circ$
			$\circ\circ\circ\circ\circ$
			$\circ\circ\circ\circ\circ$
			$\circ\circ\circ\circ\circ$
			$\circ\circ\circ\circ\circ$
			$\circ\circ\circ\circ\circ$
			$\circ\circ\circ\circ\circ$
			$\circ\circ\circ\circ\circ$
			$\circ\circ\circ\circ\circ$
			$\circ\circ\circ\circ\circ$
			$\circ\circ\circ\circ\circ$
			$\circ\circ\circ\circ\circ$

Date & Time	Subject	Category	Importance
			○ ○ ○ ○ ○
			○ ○ ○ ○ ○
			○ ○ ○ ○ ○
			○ ○ ○ ○ ○
			○ ○ ○ ○ ○
			○ ○ ○ ○ ○
			○ ○ ○ ○ ○
			○ ○ ○ ○ ○
			○ ○ ○ ○ ○
			○ ○ ○ ○ ○
			○ ○ ○ ○ ○
			○ ○ ○ ○ ○
			○ ○ ○ ○ ○
			○ ○ ○ ○ ○
			○ ○ ○ ○ ○
			○ ○ ○ ○ ○
			○ ○ ○ ○ ○
			○ ○ ○ ○ ○

Date & Time	Subject	Category	Importance
			○ ○ ○ ○ ○
			○ ○ ○ ○ ○
			○ ○ ○ ○ ○
			○ ○ ○ ○ ○
			○ ○ ○ ○ ○
			○ ○ ○ ○ ○
			○ ○ ○ ○ ○
			○ ○ ○ ○ ○
			○ ○ ○ ○ ○
			○ ○ ○ ○ ○
			○ ○ ○ ○ ○
			○ ○ ○ ○ ○
			○ ○ ○ ○ ○
			○ ○ ○ ○ ○
			○ ○ ○ ○ ○
			○ ○ ○ ○ ○
			○ ○ ○ ○ ○
			○ ○ ○ ○ ○

Date & Time	Subject	Category	Importance
			○ ○ ○ ○ ○
			○ ○ ○ ○ ○
			○ ○ ○ ○ ○
			○ ○ ○ ○ ○
			○ ○ ○ ○ ○
			○ ○ ○ ○ ○
			○ ○ ○ ○ ○
			○ ○ ○ ○ ○
			○ ○ ○ ○ ○
			○ ○ ○ ○ ○
	Love is nuthin' but a cramp of the heart		○ ○ ○ ○ ○
			○ ○ ○ ○ ○
			○ ○ ○ ○ ○
			○ ○ ○ ○ ○
			○ ○ ○ ○ ○
			○ ○ ○ ○ ○
			○ ○ ○ ○ ○
			○ ○ ○ ○ ○

99

Date & Time	Subject	Category	Importance
			○○○○○
			○○○○○
			○○○○○
			○○○○○
			○○○○○
			○○○○○
			○○○○○
			○○○○○
			○○○○○
			○○○○○
			○○○○○
			○○○○○
			○○○○○
			○○○○○
			○○○○○
			○○○○○
			○○○○○
			○○○○○

Date & Time	Subject	Category	Importance
			○○○○○
			○○○○○
			○○○○○
			○○○○○
			○○○○○
			○○○○○
			○○○○○
			○○○○○
			○○○○○
			○○○○○
			○○○○○
			○○○○○
			○○○○○
			○○○○○
			○○○○○
			○○○○○
			○○○○○
			○○○○○

STOP
CAPITALIZING
ON MY FEELINGS

Date	Subject	Category	Importance
			○ ○ ○ ○ ○
			○ ○ ○ ○ ○
			○ ○ ○ ○ ○
			○ ○ ○ ○ ○
			○ ○ ○ ○ ○
			○ ○ ○ ○ ○
			○ ○ ○ ○ ○
			○ ○ ○ ○ ○
			○ ○ ○ ○ ○
			○ ○ ○ ○ ○
			○ ○ ○ ○ ○
			○ ○ ○ ○ ○
			○ ○ ○ ○ ○
			○ ○ ○ ○ ○
			○ ○ ○ ○ ○
			○ ○ ○ ○ ○
			○ ○ ○ ○ ○
			○ ○ ○ ○ ○

I LUV U
U LUV ME
SO LET'S DO IT

Date	Subject	Category	Importance
			○ ○ ○ ○ ○
			○ ○ ○ ○ ○
			○ ○ ○ ○ ○
			○ ○ ○ ○ ○
			○ ○ ○ ○ ○
			○ ○ ○ ○ ○
			○ ○ ○ ○ ○
			○ ○ ○ ○ ○
			○ ○ ○ ○ ○
			○ ○ ○ ○ ○
			○ ○ ○ ○ ○
			○ ○ ○ ○ ○
			○ ○ ○ ○ ○
			○ ○ ○ ○ ○
			○ ○ ○ ○ ○
			○ ○ ○ ○ ○
			○ ○ ○ ○ ○
			○ ○ ○ ○ ○

Date & Time	Subject	Category	Importance
			$\circ\circ\circ\circ\circ$
			$\circ\circ\circ\circ\circ$
			$\circ\circ\circ\circ\circ$
			$\circ\circ\circ\circ\circ$
			$\circ\circ\circ\circ\circ$
			$\circ\circ\circ\circ\circ$
			$\circ\circ\circ\circ\circ$
			$\circ\circ\circ\circ\circ$
			$\circ\circ\circ\circ\circ$
			$\circ\circ\circ\circ\circ$
			$\circ\circ\circ\circ\circ$
			$\circ\circ\circ\circ\circ$
			$\circ\circ\circ\circ\circ$
			$\circ\circ\circ\circ\circ$
			$\circ\circ\circ\circ\circ$
			$\circ\circ\circ\circ\circ$
			$\circ\circ\circ\circ\circ$
			$\circ\circ\circ\circ\circ$

Date & Time	Subject	Category	Importance
			○ ○ ○ ○ ○
			○ ○ ○ ○ ○
			○ ○ ○ ○ ○
			○ ○ ○ ○ ○
			○ ○ ○ ○ ○
			○ ○ ○ ○ ○
			○ ○ ○ ○ ○
			○ ○ ○ ○ ○
			○ ○ ○ ○ ○
			○ ○ ○ ○ ○
			○ ○ ○ ○ ○
			○ ○ ○ ○ ○
			○ ○ ○ ○ ○
			○ ○ ○ ○ ○
			○ ○ ○ ○ ○
			○ ○ ○ ○ ○
			○ ○ ○ ○ ○
			○ ○ ○ ○ ○

Date & Time	Subject	Category	Importance
			○ ○ ○ ○ ○
			○ ○ ○ ○ ○
			○ ○ ○ ○ ○
			○ ○ ○ ○ ○
			○ ○ ○ ○ ○
			○ ○ ○ ○ ○
			○ ○ ○ ○ ○
	I miss you so much I could die!		○ ○ ○ ○ ○
			○ ○ ○ ○ ○
			○ ○ ○ ○ ○
			○ ○ ○ ○ ○
			○ ○ ○ ○ ○
			○ ○ ○ ○ ○
			○ ○ ○ ○ ○
			○ ○ ○ ○ ○
			○ ○ ○ ○ ○
			○ ○ ○ ○ ○
			○ ○ ○ ○ ○

Date & Time	Subject	Category	Importance
			○ ○ ○ ○ ○
			○ ○ ○ ○ ○
			○ ○ ○ ○ ○
			○ ○ ○ ○ ○
			○ ○ ○ ○ ○
			○ ○ ○ ○ ○
			○ ○ ○ ○ ○
	I miss you too honey-bunny, but hey, as soon as the big couple are done with this spread we will be together again!		○ ○ ○ ○ ○
			○ ○ ○ ○ ○
			○ ○ ○ ○ ○
			○ ○ ○ ○ ○
			○ ○ ○ ○ ○
			○ ○ ○ ○ ○
			○ ○ ○ ○ ○
			○ ○ ○ ○ ○
			○ ○ ○ ○ ○
			○ ○ ○ ○ ○
			○ ○ ○ ○ ○

Date & Time	Subject	Category	Importance
			○ ○ ○ ○ ○
			○ ○ ○ ○ ○
			○ ○ ○ ○ ○
			○ ○ ○ ○ ○
			○ ○ ○ ○ ○
			○ ○ ○ ○ ○
			○ ○ ○ ○ ○
			○ ○ ○ ○ ○
			○ ○ ○ ○ ○
			○ ○ ○ ○ ○
			○ ○ ○ ○ ○
			○ ○ ○ ○ ○
			○ ○ ○ ○ ○
			○ ○ ○ ○ ○
			○ ○ ○ ○ ○
			○ ○ ○ ○ ○
			○ ○ ○ ○ ○
			○ ○ ○ ○ ○

Date & Time	Subject	Category	Importance
			○ ○ ○ ○ ○
			○ ○ ○ ○ ○
			○ ○ ○ ○ ○
			○ ○ ○ ○ ○
			○ ○ ○ ○ ○
			○ ○ ○ ○ ○
			○ ○ ○ ○ ○
			○ ○ ○ ○ ○
			○ ○ ○ ○ ○
			○ ○ ○ ○ ○
			○ ○ ○ ○ ○
			○ ○ ○ ○ ○
			○ ○ ○ ○ ○
			○ ○ ○ ○ ○
			○ ○ ○ ○ ○
			○ ○ ○ ○ ○
			○ ○ ○ ○ ○
			○ ○ ○ ○ ○

Date & Time	Subject	Category	Importance
			○ ○ ○ ○ ○
			○ ○ ○ ○ ○
			○ ○ ○ ○ ○
			○ ○ ○ ○ ○
			○ ○ ○ ○ ○
			○ ○ ○ ○ ○
			○ ○ ○ ○ ○
			○ ○ ○ ○ ○
			○ ○ ○ ○ ○
			○ ○ ○ ○ ○
			○ ○ ○ ○ ○
			○ ○ ○ ○ ○
			○ ○ ○ ○ ○
			○ ○ ○ ○ ○
			○ ○ ○ ○ ○
			○ ○ ○ ○ ○
			○ ○ ○ ○ ○
			○ ○ ○ ○ ○

Date & Time	Subject	Category	Importance
			○ ○ ○ ○ ○
			○ ○ ○ ○ ○
			○ ○ ○ ○ ○
			○ ○ ○ ○ ○
			○ ○ ○ ○ ○
			○ ○ ○ ○ ○
			○ ○ ○ ○ ○
			○ ○ ○ ○ ○
			○ ○ ○ ○ ○
			○ ○ ○ ○ ○
			○ ○ ○ ○ ○
			○ ○ ○ ○ ○
			○ ○ ○ ○ ○
			○ ○ ○ ○ ○
			○ ○ ○ ○ ○
			○ ○ ○ ○ ○
			○ ○ ○ ○ ○
			○ ○ ○ ○ ○

Date & Time	Subject	Category	Importance
			○ ○ ○ ○ ○
			○ ○ ○ ○ ○
			○ ○ ○ ○ ○
			○ ○ ○ ○ ○
			○ ○ ○ ○ ○
			○ ○ ○ ○ ○
			○ ○ ○ ○ ○
			○ ○ ○ ○ ○
			○ ○ ○ ○ ○
			○ ○ ○ ○ ○
			○ ○ ○ ○ ○
			○ ○ ○ ○ ○
			○ ○ ○ ○ ○
			○ ○ ○ ○ ○
			○ ○ ○ ○ ○
			○ ○ ○ ○ ○
			○ ○ ○ ○ ○
			○ ○ ○ ○ ○

Date & Time	Subject	Category	Importance
			○ ○ ○ ○ ○
			○ ○ ○ ○ ○
			○ ○ ○ ○ ○
			○ ○ ○ ○ ○
			○ ○ ○ ○ ○
			○ ○ ○ ○ ○
			○ ○ ○ ○ ○
			○ ○ ○ ○ ○
			○ ○ ○ ○ ○
			○ ○ ○ ○ ○
			○ ○ ○ ○ ○
			○ ○ ○ ○ ○
			○ ○ ○ ○ ○
			○ ○ ○ ○ ○
			○ ○ ○ ○ ○
			○ ○ ○ ○ ○
			○ ○ ○ ○ ○
			○ ○ ○ ○ ○

Date & Time	Subject	Category	Importance
			○ ○ ○ ○ ○
			○ ○ ○ ○ ○
			○ ○ ○ ○ ○
			○ ○ ○ ○ ○
			○ ○ ○ ○ ○
			○ ○ ○ ○ ○
			○ ○ ○ ○ ○
			○ ○ ○ ○ ○
			○ ○ ○ ○ ○
	If you find love, please return it to Emily Barwick, 12 Poppy Lane		○ ○ ○ ○ ○
			○ ○ ○ ○ ○
			○ ○ ○ ○ ○
			○ ○ ○ ○ ○
			○ ○ ○ ○ ○
			○ ○ ○ ○ ○
			○ ○ ○ ○ ○
			○ ○ ○ ○ ○
			○ ○ ○ ○ ○

Date & Time	Subject	Category	Importance
			○ ○ ○ ○ ○
			○ ○ ○ ○ ○
			○ ○ ○ ○ ○
			○ ○ ○ ○ ○
			○ ○ ○ ○ ○
			○ ○ ○ ○ ○
			○ ○ ○ ○ ○
			○ ○ ○ ○ ○
			○ ○ ○ ○ ○
			○ ○ ○ ○ ○
			○ ○ ○ ○ ○
			○ ○ ○ ○ ○
			○ ○ ○ ○ ○
			○ ○ ○ ○ ○
			○ ○ ○ ○ ○
			○ ○ ○ ○ ○
			○ ○ ○ ○ ○
			○ ○ ○ ○ ○

Date & Time	Subject	Category	Importance
			○ ○ ○ ○ ○
			○ ○ ○ ○ ○
			○ ○ ○ ○ ○
			○ ○ ○ ○ ○
			○ ○ ○ ○ ○
			○ ○ ○ ○ ○
			○ ○ ○ ○ ○
			○ ○ ○ ○ ○
			○ ○ ○ ○ ○
			○ ○ ○ ○ ○
			○ ○ ○ ○ ○
			○ ○ ○ ○ ○
			○ ○ ○ ○ ○
			○ ○ ○ ○ ○
			○ ○ ○ ○ ○
			○ ○ ○ ○ ○
			○ ○ ○ ○ ○
			○ ○ ○ ○ ○

Date & Time	Subject	Category	Importance
			○ ○ ○ ○ ○
			○ ○ ○ ○ ○
			○ ○ ○ ○ ○
			○ ○ ○ ○ ○
			○ ○ ○ ○ ○
			○ ○ ○ ○ ○
			○ ○ ○ ○ ○
			○ ○ ○ ○ ○
			○ ○ ○ ○ ○
			○ ○ ○ ○ ○
			○ ○ ○ ○ ○
			○ ○ ○ ○ ○
			○ ○ ○ ○ ○
			○ ○ ○ ○ ○
			○ ○ ○ ○ ○
			○ ○ ○ ○ ○
			○ ○ ○ ○ ○
			○ ○ ○ ○ ○

Date & Time	Subject	Category	Importance
			○ ○ ○ ○ ○
			○ ○ ○ ○ ○
			○ ○ ○ ○ ○
			○ ○ ○ ○ ○
			○ ○ ○ ○ ○
			○ ○ ○ ○ ○
			○ ○ ○ ○ ○
			○ ○ ○ ○ ○
			○ ○ ○ ○ ○
			○ ○ ○ ○ ○
			○ ○ ○ ○ ○
			○ ○ ○ ○ ○
			○ ○ ○ ○ ○
			○ ○ ○ ○ ○
			○ ○ ○ ○ ○
			○ ○ ○ ○ ○
			○ ○ ○ ○ ○
			○ ○ ○ ○ ○

Date & Time	Subject	Category	Importance
			○ ○ ○ ○ ○
			○ ○ ○ ○ ○
			○ ○ ○ ○ ○
			○ ○ ○ ○ ○
			○ ○ ○ ○ ○
			○ ○ ○ ○ ○
			○ ○ ○ ○ ○
			○ ○ ○ ○ ○
			○ ○ ○ ○ ○
			○ ○ ○ ○ ○
			○ ○ ○ ○ ○
			○ ○ ○ ○ ○
			○ ○ ○ ○ ○
			○ ○ ○ ○ ○
			○ ○ ○ ○ ○
			○ ○ ○ ○ ○
			○ ○ ○ ○ ○
			○ ○ ○ ○ ○

We both had a sex change just so we could be together...

Date & Time	Subject	Category	Importance
			○ ○ ○ ○ ○
			○ ○ ○ ○ ○
			○ ○ ○ ○ ○
			○ ○ ○ ○ ○
			○ ○ ○ ○ ○
			○ ○ ○ ○ ○
			○ ○ ○ ○ ○
			○ ○ ○ ○ ○
			○ ○ ○ ○ ○
			○ ○ ○ ○ ○
			○ ○ ○ ○ ○
			○ ○ ○ ○ ○
			○ ○ ○ ○ ○
			○ ○ ○ ○ ○
			○ ○ ○ ○ ○
			○ ○ ○ ○ ○
			○ ○ ○ ○ ○

Date & Time	Subject	Category	Importance
			○ ○ ○ ○ ○
			○ ○ ○ ○ ○
			○ ○ ○ ○ ○
			○ ○ ○ ○ ○
			○ ○ ○ ○ ○
			○ ○ ○ ○ ○
			○ ○ ○ ○ ○
			○ ○ ○ ○ ○
			○ ○ ○ ○ ○
			○ ○ ○ ○ ○
			○ ○ ○ ○ ○
			○ ○ ○ ○ ○
			○ ○ ○ ○ ○
			○ ○ ○ ○ ○
			○ ○ ○ ○ ○
			○ ○ ○ ○ ○
			○ ○ ○ ○ ○
			○ ○ ○ ○ ○

Date & Time	Subject	Category	Importance
			○ ○ ○ ○ ○
			○ ○ ○ ○ ○
			○ ○ ○ ○ ○
			○ ○ ○ ○ ○
			○ ○ ○ ○ ○
			○ ○ ○ ○ ○
			○ ○ ○ ○ ○
			○ ○ ○ ○ ○
			○ ○ ○ ○ ○
			○ ○ ○ ○ ○
			○ ○ ○ ○ ○
			○ ○ ○ ○ ○
			○ ○ ○ ○ ○
			○ ○ ○ ○ ○
			○ ○ ○ ○ ○
			○ ○ ○ ○ ○
			○ ○ ○ ○ ○
			○ ○ ○ ○ ○

Date & Time	Subject	Category	Importance
			○ ○ ○ ○ ○
			○ ○ ○ ○ ○
			○ ○ ○ ○ ○
			○ ○ ○ ○ ○
			○ ○ ○ ○ ○
			○ ○ ○ ○ ○
			○ ○ ○ ○ ○
			○ ○ ○ ○ ○
			○ ○ ○ ○ ○
			○ ○ ○ ○ ○
			○ ○ ○ ○ ○
			○ ○ ○ ○ ○
			○ ○ ○ ○ ○
			○ ○ ○ ○ ○
			○ ○ ○ ○ ○
			○ ○ ○ ○ ○
			○ ○ ○ ○ ○

HEY! I OWE SOME MONEY TO THE GUY ON PAGE 98 AND SOME TO THE DUDE ON PAGE 113. CAN YOU PAY THEM AND I'LL OWE YOU INSTEAD? ITS JUST A BIT MORE CONVENIENT TO HAVE ALL MY DEBTS IN ONE PLACE. I WILL PAY YOU BACK (SOMETIMES)

Date & Time	Subject	Category	Importance
			○ ○ ○ ○ ○
			○ ○ ○ ○ ○
			○ ○ ○ ○ ○
			○ ○ ○ ○ ○
			○ ○ ○ ○ ○
			○ ○ ○ ○ ○
			○ ○ ○ ○ ○
			○ ○ ○ ○ ○
			○ ○ ○ ○ ○
			○ ○ ○ ○ ○
			○ ○ ○ ○ ○
			○ ○ ○ ○ ○
			○ ○ ○ ○ ○
			○ ○ ○ ○ ○
			○ ○ ○ ○ ○
			○ ○ ○ ○ ○
			○ ○ ○ ○ ○
			○ ○ ○ ○ ○

Date & Time	Subject	Category	Importance
			○ ○ ○ ○ ○
			○ ○ ○ ○ ○
			○ ○ ○ ○ ○
			○ ○ ○ ○ ○
			○ ○ ○ ○ ○
			○ ○ ○ ○ ○
			○ ○ ○ ○ ○
			○ ○ ○ ○ ○
			○ ○ ○ ○ ○
			○ ○ ○ ○ ○
			○ ○ ○ ○ ○
			○ ○ ○ ○ ○
			○ ○ ○ ○ ○
			○ ○ ○ ○ ○
			○ ○ ○ ○ ○
			○ ○ ○ ○ ○
			○ ○ ○ ○ ○
			○ ○ ○ ○ ○

Date & Time	Subject	Category	Importance
			○ ○ ○ ○ ○
			○ ○ ○ ○ ○
			○ ○ ○ ○ ○
			○ ○ ○ ○ ○
			○ ○ ○ ○ ○
			○ ○ ○ ○ ○
			○ ○ ○ ○ ○
			○ ○ ○ ○ ○
			○ ○ ○ ○ ○
			○ ○ ○ ○ ○
			○ ○ ○ ○ ○
			○ ○ ○ ○ ○
			○ ○ ○ ○ ○
			○ ○ ○ ○ ○
			○ ○ ○ ○ ○
			○ ○ ○ ○ ○
			○ ○ ○ ○ ○
			○ ○ ○ ○ ○

Date & Time	Subject	Category	Importance
			○ ○ ○ ○ ○
			○ ○ ○ ○ ○
			○ ○ ○ ○ ○
			○ ○ ○ ○ ○
			○ ○ ○ ○ ○
			○ ○ ○ ○ ○
			○ ○ ○ ○ ○
			○ ○ ○ ○ ○
			○ ○ ○ ○ ○
			○ ○ ○ ○ ○
			○ ○ ○ ○ ○
			○ ○ ○ ○ ○
			○ ○ ○ ○ ○
			○ ○ ○ ○ ○
			○ ○ ○ ○ ○
			○ ○ ○ ○ ○
			○ ○ ○ ○ ○
			○ ○ ○ ○ ○

Date & Time	Subject	Category	Importance
			○ ○ ○ ○ ○
			○ ○ ○ ○ ○
			○ ○ ○ ○ ○
			○ ○ ○ ○ ○
			○ ○ ○ ○ ○
			○ ○ ○ ○ ○
			○ ○ ○ ○ ○
			○ ○ ○ ○ ○
			○ ○ ○ ○ ○
			○ ○ ○ ○ ○
			○ ○ ○ ○ ○
			○ ○ ○ ○ ○
			○ ○ ○ ○ ○
			○ ○ ○ ○ ○
			○ ○ ○ ○ ○
			○ ○ ○ ○ ○
			○ ○ ○ ○ ○
			○ ○ ○ ○ ○

Date & Time	Subject	Category	Importance
			○ ○ ○ ○ ○
			○ ○ ○ ○ ○
			○ ○ ○ ○ ○
			○ ○ ○ ○ ○
			○ ○ ○ ○ ○
			○ ○ ○ ○ ○
			○ ○ ○ ○ ○
			○ ○ ○ ○ ○
			○ ○ ○ ○ ○
			○ ○ ○ ○ ○
			○ ○ ○ ○ ○
			○ ○ ○ ○ ○
			○ ○ ○ ○ ○
			○ ○ ○ ○ ○
			○ ○ ○ ○ ○
			○ ○ ○ ○ ○
			○ ○ ○ ○ ○
			○ ○ ○ ○ ○

Date & Time	Subject	Category	Importance
			○○○○○
			○○○○○
			○○○○○
			○○○○○
			○○○○○
			○○○○○
			○○○○○
			○○○○○
			○○○○○
			○○○○○
			○○○○○
			○○○○○
			○○○○○
			○○○○○
			○○○○○
			○○○○○
			○○○○○
			○○○○○

ONCE WHEN I WERE IN A RESTAURANT I WERE COMPLIMENTED BY ONE OF THE OTHER GUESTS.

Date & Time	Subject	Category	Importance
			○ ○ ○ ○ ○
			○ ○ ○ ○ ○
			○ ○ ○ ○ ○
			○ ○ ○ ○ ○
			○ ○ ○ ○ ○
			○ ○ ○ ○ ○
			○ ○ ○ ○ ○
			○ ○ ○ ○ ○
			○ ○ ○ ○ ○
			○ ○ ○ ○ ○
			○ ○ ○ ○ ○
			○ ○ ○ ○ ○
			○ ○ ○ ○ ○
			○ ○ ○ ○ ○
			○ ○ ○ ○ ○
			○ ○ ○ ○ ○
			○ ○ ○ ○ ○
			○ ○ ○ ○ ○

Date & Time	Subject	Category	Importance
			○ ○ ○ ○ ○
			○ ○ ○ ○ ○
			○ ○ ○ ○ ○
			○ ○ ○ ○ ○
			○ ○ ○ ○ ○
			○ ○ ○ ○ ○
			○ ○ ○ ○ ○
			○ ○ ○ ○ ○
			○ ○ ○ ○ ○
			○ ○ ○ ○ ○
			○ ○ ○ ○ ○
			○ ○ ○ ○ ○
			○ ○ ○ ○ ○
			○ ○ ○ ○ ○
			○ ○ ○ ○ ○
			○ ○ ○ ○ ○
			○ ○ ○ ○ ○
			○ ○ ○ ○ ○

Date & Time	Subject	Category	Importance
			○ ○ ○ ○ ○
			○ ○ ○ ○ ○
			○ ○ ○ ○ ○
			○ ○ ○ ○ ○
			○ ○ ○ ○ ○
			○ ○ ○ ○ ○
			○ ○ ○ ○ ○
			○ ○ ○ ○ ○
			○ ○ ○ ○ ○
			○ ○ ○ ○ ○
			○ ○ ○ ○ ○
			○ ○ ○ ○ ○
			○ ○ ○ ○ ○
			○ ○ ○ ○ ○
			○ ○ ○ ○ ○
			○ ○ ○ ○ ○
			○ ○ ○ ○ ○
			○ ○ ○ ○ ○

I USE THIS DESK TO WORK AT MY RELATIONSHIP

Date & Time	Subject	Category	Importance
			○ ○ ○ ○ ○
			○ ○ ○ ○ ○
			○ ○ ○ ○ ○
			○ ○ ○ ○ ○
			○ ○ ○ ○ ○
			○ ○ ○ ○ ○
			○ ○ ○ ○ ○
			○ ○ ○ ○ ○
			○ ○ ○ ○ ○
			○ ○ ○ ○ ○
			○ ○ ○ ○ ○
			○ ○ ○ ○ ○
			○ ○ ○ ○ ○
			○ ○ ○ ○ ○
			○ ○ ○ ○ ○
			○ ○ ○ ○ ○
			○ ○ ○ ○ ○
			○ ○ ○ ○ ○

Date & Time	Subject	Category	Importance
			○ ○ ○ ○ ○
			○ ○ ○ ○ ○
			○ ○ ○ ○ ○
			○ ○ ○ ○ ○
			○ ○ ○ ○ ○
			○ ○ ○ ○ ○
			○ ○ ○ ○ ○
			○ ○ ○ ○ ○
			○ ○ ○ ○ ○
			○ ○ ○ ○ ○
			○ ○ ○ ○ ○
			○ ○ ○ ○ ○
			○ ○ ○ ○ ○
			○ ○ ○ ○ ○
			○ ○ ○ ○ ○
			○ ○ ○ ○ ○
			○ ○ ○ ○ ○
			○ ○ ○ ○ ○

I DON'T WANT YOU TO TREAT ME AS A ONE DAY THING. I WANT YOU TO COME BACK AND PAT MY FACE EVERY DAY OF THE NEXT YEAR I LOVE YOU AND I AM YOUR BEST FRIEND.

Date & Time	Subject	Category	Importance
			○ ○ ○ ○ ○
			○ ○ ○ ○ ○
			○ ○ ○ ○ ○
			○ ○ ○ ○ ○
			○ ○ ○ ○ ○
			○ ○ ○ ○ ○
			○ ○ ○ ○ ○
			○ ○ ○ ○ ○
			○ ○ ○ ○ ○
			○ ○ ○ ○ ○
			○ ○ ○ ○ ○
			○ ○ ○ ○ ○
			○ ○ ○ ○ ○
			○ ○ ○ ○ ○
			○ ○ ○ ○ ○
			○ ○ ○ ○ ○
			○ ○ ○ ○ ○
			○ ○ ○ ○ ○

Date & Time	Subject	Category	Importance
			○ ○ ○ ○ ○
			○ ○ ○ ○ ○
			○ ○ ○ ○ ○
			○ ○ ○ ○ ○
			○ ○ ○ ○ ○
			○ ○ ○ ○ ○
			○ ○ ○ ○ ○
			○ ○ ○ ○ ○
			○ ○ ○ ○ ○
			○ ○ ○ ○ ○
			○ ○ ○ ○ ○
			○ ○ ○ ○ ○
			○ ○ ○ ○ ○
			○ ○ ○ ○ ○
			○ ○ ○ ○ ○
			○ ○ ○ ○ ○
			○ ○ ○ ○ ○
			○ ○ ○ ○ ○

So where the hell are the etchings?

137

Date & Time	Subject	Category	Importance
			○○○○○
			○○○○○
			○○○○○
			○○○○○
			○○○○○
			○○○○○
			○○○○○
			○○○○○
			○○○○○
			○○○○○
			○○○○○
			○○○○○
			○○○○○
			○○○○○
			○○○○○
			○○○○○
			○○○○○
			○○○○○

BENRIK ♡ YOU

Date & Time	Subject	Category	Importance
			○ ○ ○ ○ ○
			○ ○ ○ ○ ○
			○ ○ ○ ○ ○
			○ ○ ○ ○ ○
			○ ○ ○ ○ ○
			○ ○ ○ ○ ○
			○ ○ ○ ○ ○
			○ ○ ○ ○ ○
			○ ○ ○ ○ ○
			○ ○ ○ ○ ○
			○ ○ ○ ○ ○
			○ ○ ○ ○ ○
			○ ○ ○ ○ ○
			○ ○ ○ ○ ○
			○ ○ ○ ○ ○
			○ ○ ○ ○ ○
			○ ○ ○ ○ ○
			○ ○ ○ ○ ○

Things I Know About You

True intimacy is hard work. In this chapter you are to write about each other. How well do you know your partner? From your life stories to your secrets, this is the chance to explore and expose your unparalleled knowledge of each other's inner workings.

Important dates

Long-term relationships are defined by key dates, milestones of coupledom. Record the dates that matter to each other, then circle them in the 30-year calendar opposite to ensure they're not forgotten.

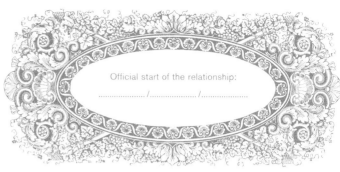

Official start of the relationship:

.... / .... / ....

Official proposal day:

.... / .... / ....

Official acceptance day (if different):

.... / .... / ....

Official wedding day:

.... /

.... /

....

Her birthday:

.... / .... / ....

His birthday:

.... / .... / ....

Kid's birthday:

.... / .... / ....

2005

January
1 2 3 4 5 6 7 8
9 10 11 12 13 14 15 16
17 18 19 20 21 22 23 24
25 26 27 28 29 30 31

February
1 2 3 4 5 6 7 8
9 10 11 12 13 14 15 16
17 18 19 20 21 22 23 24
25 26 27 28

March
1 2 3 4 5 6 7 8
9 10 11 12 13 14 15 16
17 18 19 20 21 22 23 24
25 26 27 28 29 30 31

April
1 2 3 4 5 6 7 8
9 10 11 12 13 14 15 16
17 18 19 20 21 22 23 24
25 26 27 28 29 30

May
1 2 3 4 5 6 7 8
9 10 11 12 13 14 15 16
17 18 19 20 21 22 23 24
25 26 27 28 29 30 31

June
1 2 3 4 5 6 7 8
9 10 11 12 13 14 15 16
17 18 19 20 21 22 23 24
25 26 27 28 29 30

July
1 2 3 4 5 6 7 8
9 10 11 12 13 14 15 16
17 18 19 20 21 22 23 24
25 26 27 28 29 30 31

August
1 2 3 4 5 6 7 8
9 10 11 12 13 14 15 16
17 18 19 20 21 22 23 24
25 26 27 28 29 30 31

September
1 2 3 4 5 6 7 8
9 10 11 12 13 14 15 16
17 18 19 20 21 22 23 24
25 26 27 28 29 30

October
1 2 3 4 5 6 7 8
9 10 11 12 13 14 15 16
17 18 19 20 21 22 23 24
25 26 27 28 29 30 31

November
1 2 3 4 5 6 7 8
9 10 11 12 13 14 15 16
17 18 19 20 21 22 23 24
25 26 27 28 29 30

December
1 2 3 4 5 6 7 8
9 10 11 12 13 14 15 16
17 18 19 20 21 22 23 24
25 26 27 28 29 30 31

2006

January
1 2 3 4 5 6 7 8
9 10 11 12 13 14 15 16
17 18 19 20 21 22 23 24
25 26 27 28 29 30 31

February
1 2 3 4 5 6 7 8
9 10 11 12 13 14 15 16
17 18 19 20 21 22 23 24
25 26 27 28

March
1 2 3 4 5 6 7 8
9 10 11 12 13 14 15 16
17 18 19 20 21 22 23 24
25 26 27 28 29 30 31

April
1 2 3 4 5 6 7 8
9 10 11 12 13 14 15 16
17 18 19 20 21 22 23 24
25 26 27 28 29 30

May
1 2 3 4 5 6 7 8
9 10 11 12 13 14 15 16
17 18 19 20 21 22 23 24
25 26 27 28 29 30 31

June
1 2 3 4 5 6 7 8
9 10 11 12 13 14 15 16
17 18 19 20 21 22 23 24
25 26 27 28 29 30

July
1 2 3 4 5 6 7 8
9 10 11 12 13 14 15 16
17 18 19 20 21 22 23 24
25 26 27 28 29 30 31

August
1 2 3 4 5 6 7 8
9 10 11 12 13 14 15 16
17 18 19 20 21 22 23 24
25 26 27 28 29 30 31

September
1 2 3 4 5 6 7 8
9 10 11 12 13 14 15 16
17 18 19 20 21 22 23 24
25 26 27 28 29 30

October
1 2 3 4 5 6 7 8
9 10 11 12 13 14 15 16
17 18 19 20 21 22 23 24
25 26 27 28 29 30 31

November
1 2 3 4 5 6 7 8
9 10 11 12 13 14 15 16
17 18 19 20 21 22 23 24
25 26 27 28 29 30

December
1 2 3 4 5 6 7 8
9 10 11 12 13 14 15 16
17 18 19 20 21 22 23 24
25 26 27 28 29 30 31

2007

January
1 2 3 4 5 6 7 8
9 10 11 12 13 14 15 16
17 18 19 20 21 22 23 24
25 26 27 28 29 30 31

February
1 2 3 4 5 6 7 8
9 10 11 12 13 14 15 16
17 18 19 20 21 22 23 24
25 26 27 28

March
1 2 3 4 5 6 7 8
9 10 11 12 13 14 15 16
17 18 19 20 21 22 23 24
25 26 27 28 29 30 31

April
1 2 3 4 5 6 7 8
9 10 11 12 13 14 15 16
17 18 19 20 21 22 23 24
25 26 27 28 29 30

May
1 2 3 4 5 6 7 8
9 10 11 12 13 14 15 16
17 18 19 20 21 22 23 24
25 26 27 28 29 30 31

June
1 2 3 4 5 6 7 8
9 10 11 12 13 14 15 16
17 18 19 20 21 22 23 24
25 26 27 28 29 30

July
1 2 3 4 5 6 7 8
9 10 11 12 13 14 15 16
17 18 19 20 21 22 23 24
25 26 27 28 29 30 31

August
1 2 3 4 5 6 7 8
9 10 11 12 13 14 15 16
17 18 19 20 21 22 23 24
25 26 27 28 29 30 31

September
1 2 3 4 5 6 7 8
9 10 11 12 13 14 15 16
17 18 19 20 21 22 23 24
25 26 27 28 29 30

October
1 2 3 4 5 6 7 8
9 10 11 12 13 14 15 16
17 18 19 20 21 22 23 24
25 26 27 28 29 30 31

November
1 2 3 4 5 6 7 8
9 10 11 12 13 14 15 16
17 18 19 20 21 22 23 24
25 26 27 28 29 30

December
1 2 3 4 5 6 7 8
9 10 11 12 13 14 15 16
17 18 19 20 21 22 23 24
25 26 27 28 29 30 31

2008

January
1 2 3 4 5 6 7 8
9 10 11 12 13 14 15 16
17 18 19 20 21 22 23 24
25 26 27 28 29 30 31

February
1 2 3 4 5 6 7 8
9 10 11 12 13 14 15 16
17 18 19 20 21 22 23 24
25 26 27 28 29

March
1 2 3 4 5 6 7 8
9 10 11 12 13 14 15 16
17 18 19 20 21 22 23 24
25 26 27 28 29 30 31

April
1 2 3 4 5 6 7 8
9 10 11 12 13 14 15 16
17 18 19 20 21 22 23 24
25 26 27 28 29 30

May
1 2 3 4 5 6 7 8
9 10 11 12 13 14 15 16
17 18 19 20 21 22 23 24
25 26 27 28 29 30 31

June
1 2 3 4 5 6 7 8
9 10 11 12 13 14 15 16
17 18 19 20 21 22 23 24
25 26 27 28 29 30

July
1 2 3 4 5 6 7 8
9 10 11 12 13 14 15 16
17 18 19 20 21 22 23 24
25 26 27 28 29 30 31

August
1 2 3 4 5 6 7 8
9 10 11 12 13 14 15 16
17 18 19 20 21 22 23 24
25 26 27 28 29 30 31

September
1 2 3 4 5 6 7 8
9 10 11 12 13 14 15 16
17 18 19 20 21 22 23 24
25 26 27 28 29 30

October
1 2 3 4 5 6 7 8
9 10 11 12 13 14 15 16
17 18 19 20 21 22 23 24
25 26 27 28 29 30 31

November
1 2 3 4 5 6 7 8
9 10 11 12 13 14 15 16
17 18 19 20 21 22 23 24
25 26 27 28 29 30

December
1 2 3 4 5 6 7 8
9 10 11 12 13 14 15 16
17 18 19 20 21 22 23 24
25 26 27 28 29 30 31

2009

January
1 2 3 4 5 6 7 8
9 10 11 12 13 14 15 16
17 18 19 20 21 22 23 24
25 26 27 28 29 30 31

February
1 2 3 4 5 6 7 8
9 10 11 12 13 14 15 16
17 18 19 20 21 22 23 24
25 26 27 28

March
1 2 3 4 5 6 7 8
9 10 11 12 13 14 15 16
17 18 19 20 21 22 23 24
25 26 27 28 29 30 31

April
1 2 3 4 5 6 7 8
9 10 11 12 13 14 15 16
17 18 19 20 21 22 23 24
25 26 27 28 29 30

May
1 2 3 4 5 6 7 8
9 10 11 12 13 14 15 16
17 18 19 20 21 22 23 24
25 26 27 28 29 30 31

June
1 2 3 4 5 6 7 8
9 10 11 12 13 14 15 16
17 18 19 20 21 22 23 24
25 26 27 28 29 30

July
1 2 3 4 5 6 7 8
9 10 11 12 13 14 15 16
17 18 19 20 21 22 23 24
25 26 27 28 29 30 31

August
1 2 3 4 5 6 7 8
9 10 11 12 13 14 15 16
17 18 19 20 21 22 23 24
25 26 27 28 29 30 31

September
1 2 3 4 5 6 7 8
9 10 11 12 13 14 15 16
17 18 19 20 21 22 23 24
25 26 27 28 29 30

October
1 2 3 4 5 6 7 8
9 10 11 12 13 14 15 16
17 18 19 20 21 22 23 24
25 26 27 28 29 30 31

November
1 2 3 4 5 6 7 8
9 10 11 12 13 14 15 16
17 18 19 20 21 22 23 24
25 26 27 28 29 30

December
1 2 3 4 5 6 7 8
9 10 11 12 13 14 15 16
17 18 19 20 21 22 23 24
25 26 27 28 29 30 31

2010

January
1 2 3 4 5 6 7 8
9 10 11 12 13 14 15 16
17 18 19 20 21 22 23 24
25 26 27 28 29 30 31

February
1 2 3 4 5 6 7 8
9 10 11 12 13 14 15 16
17 18 19 20 21 22 23 24
25 26 27 28

March
1 2 3 4 5 6 7 8
9 10 11 12 13 14 15 16
17 18 19 20 21 22 23 24
25 26 27 28 29 30 31

April
1 2 3 4 5 6 7 8
9 10 11 12 13 14 15 16
17 18 19 20 21 22 23 24
25 26 27 28 29 30

May
1 2 3 4 5 6 7 8
9 10 11 12 13 14 15 16
17 18 19 20 21 22 23 24
25 26 27 28 29 30 31

June
1 2 3 4 5 6 7 8
9 10 11 12 13 14 15 16
17 18 19 20 21 22 23 24
25 26 27 28 29 30

July
1 2 3 4 5 6 7 8
9 10 11 12 13 14 15 16
17 18 19 20 21 22 23 24
25 26 27 28 29 30 31

August
1 2 3 4 5 6 7 8
9 10 11 12 13 14 15 16
17 18 19 20 21 22 23 24
25 26 27 28 29 30 31

September
1 2 3 4 5 6 7 8
9 10 11 12 13 14 15 16
17 18 19 20 21 22 23 24
25 26 27 28 29 30

October
1 2 3 4 5 6 7 8
9 10 11 12 13 14 15 16
17 18 19 20 21 22 23 24
25 26 27 28 29 30 31

November
1 2 3 4 5 6 7 8
9 10 11 12 13 14 15 16
17 18 19 20 21 22 23 24
25 26 27 28 29 30

December
1 2 3 4 5 6 7 8
9 10 11 12 13 14 15 16
17 18 19 20 21 22 23 24
25 26 27 28 29 30 31

2011

January
1 2 3 4 5 6 7 8
9 10 11 12 13 14 15 16
17 18 19 20 21 22 23 24
25 26 27 28 29 30 31

February
1 2 3 4 5 6 7 8
9 10 11 12 13 14 15 16
17 18 19 20 21 22 23 24
25 26 27 28

March
1 2 3 4 5 6 7 8
9 10 11 12 13 14 15 16
17 18 19 20 21 22 23 24
25 26 27 28 29 30 31

April
1 2 3 4 5 6 7 8
9 10 11 12 13 14 15 16
17 18 19 20 21 22 23 24
25 26 27 28 29 30

May
1 2 3 4 5 6 7 8
9 10 11 12 13 14 15 16
17 18 19 20 21 22 23 24
25 26 27 28 29 30 31

June
1 2 3 4 5 6 7 8
9 10 11 12 13 14 15 16
17 18 19 20 21 22 23 24
25 26 27 28 29 30

July
1 2 3 4 5 6 7 8
9 10 11 12 13 14 15 16
17 18 19 20 21 22 23 24
25 26 27 28 29 30 31

August
1 2 3 4 5 6 7 8
9 10 11 12 13 14 15 16
17 18 19 20 21 22 23 24
25 26 27 28 29 30 31

September
1 2 3 4 5 6 7 8
9 10 11 12 13 14 15 16
17 18 19 20 21 22 23 24
25 26 27 28 29 30

October
1 2 3 4 5 6 7 8
9 10 11 12 13 14 15 16
17 18 19 20 21 22 23 24
25 26 27 28 29 30 31

November
1 2 3 4 5 6 7 8
9 10 11 12 13 14 15 16
17 18 19 20 21 22 23 24
25 26 27 28 29 30

December
1 2 3 4 5 6 7 8
9 10 11 12 13 14 15 16
17 18 19 20 21 22 23 24
25 26 27 28 29 30 31

2012

January
1 2 3 4 5 6 7 8
9 10 11 12 13 14 15 16
17 18 19 20 21 22 23 24
25 26 27 28 29 30 31

February
1 2 3 4 5 6 7 8
9 10 11 12 13 14 15 16
17 18 19 20 21 22 23 24
25 26 27 28 29

March
1 2 3 4 5 6 7 8
9 10 11 12 13 14 15 16
17 18 19 20 21 22 23 24
25 26 27 28 29 30 31

April
1 2 3 4 5 6 7 8
9 10 11 12 13 14 15 16
17 18 19 20 21 22 23 24
25 26 27 28 29 30

May
1 2 3 4 5 6 7 8
9 10 11 12 13 14 15 16
17 18 19 20 21 22 23 24
25 26 27 28 29 30 31

June
1 2 3 4 5 6 7 8
9 10 11 12 13 14 15 16
17 18 19 20 21 22 23 24
25 26 27 28 29 30

July
1 2 3 4 5 6 7 8
9 10 11 12 13 14 15 16
17 18 19 20 21 22 23 24
25 26 27 28 29 30 31

August
1 2 3 4 5 6 7 8
9 10 11 12 13 14 15 16
17 18 19 20 21 22 23 24
25 26 27 28 29 30 31

September
1 2 3 4 5 6 7 8
9 10 11 12 13 14 15 16
17 18 19 20 21 22 23 24
25 26 27 28 29 30

October
1 2 3 4 5 6 7 8
9 10 11 12 13 14 15 16
17 18 19 20 21 22 23 24
25 26 27 28 29 30 31

November
1 2 3 4 5 6 7 8
9 10 11 12 13 14 15 16
17 18 19 20 21 22 23 24
25 26 27 28 29 30

December
1 2 3 4 5 6 7 8
9 10 11 12 13 14 15 16
17 18 19 20 21 22 23 24
25 26 27 28 29 30 31

2013

January
1 2 3 4 5 6 7 8
9 10 11 12 13 14 15 16
17 18 19 20 21 22 23 24
25 26 27 28 29 30 31

February
1 2 3 4 5 6 7 8
9 10 11 12 13 14 15 16
17 18 19 20 21 22 23 24
25 26 27 28

March
1 2 3 4 5 6 7 8
9 10 11 12 13 14 15 16
17 18 19 20 21 22 23 24
25 26 27 28 29 30 31

April
1 2 3 4 5 6 7 8
9 10 11 12 13 14 15 16
17 18 19 20 21 22 23 24
25 26 27 28 29 30

May
1 2 3 4 5 6 7 8
9 10 11 12 13 14 15 16
17 18 19 20 21 22 23 24
25 26 27 28 29 30 31

June
1 2 3 4 5 6 7 8
9 10 11 12 13 14 15 16
17 18 19 20 21 22 23 24
25 26 27 28 29 30

July
1 2 3 4 5 6 7 8
9 10 11 12 13 14 15 16
17 18 19 20 21 22 23 24
25 26 27 28 29 30 31

August
1 2 3 4 5 6 7 8
9 10 11 12 13 14 15 16
17 18 19 20 21 22 23 24
25 26 27 28 29 30 31

September
1 2 3 4 5 6 7 8
9 10 11 12 13 14 15 16
17 18 19 20 21 22 23 24
25 26 27 28 29 30

October
1 2 3 4 5 6 7 8
9 10 11 12 13 14 15 16
17 18 19 20 21 22 23 24
25 26 27 28 29 30 31

November
1 2 3 4 5 6 7 8
9 10 11 12 13 14 15 16
17 18 19 20 21 22 23 24
25 26 27 28 29 30

December
1 2 3 4 5 6 7 8
9 10 11 12 13 14 15 16
17 18 19 20 21 22 23 24
25 26 27 28 29 30 31

2014

January
1 2 3 4 5 6 7 8
9 10 11 12 13 14 15 16
17 18 19 20 21 22 23 24
25 26 27 28 29 30 31

February
1 2 3 4 5 6 7 8
9 10 11 12 13 14 15 16
17 18 19 20 21 22 23 24
25 26 27 28

March
1 2 3 4 5 6 7 8
9 10 11 12 13 14 15 16
17 18 19 20 21 22 23 24
25 26 27 28 29 30 31

April
1 2 3 4 5 6 7 8
9 10 11 12 13 14 15 16
17 18 19 20 21 22 23 24
25 26 27 28 29 30

May
1 2 3 4 5 6 7 8
9 10 11 12 13 14 15 16
17 18 19 20 21 22 23 24
25 26 27 28 29 30 31

June
1 2 3 4 5 6 7 8
9 10 11 12 13 14 15 16
17 18 19 20 21 22 23 24
25 26 27 28 29 30

July
1 2 3 4 5 6 7 8
9 10 11 12 13 14 15 16
17 18 19 20 21 22 23 24
25 26 27 28 29 30 31

August
1 2 3 4 5 6 7 8
9 10 11 12 13 14 15 16
17 18 19 20 21 22 23 24
25 26 27 28 29 30 31

September
1 2 3 4 5 6 7 8
9 10 11 12 13 14 15 16
17 18 19 20 21 22 23 24
25 26 27 28 29 30

October
1 2 3 4 5 6 7 8
9 10 11 12 13 14 15 16
17 18 19 20 21 22 23 24
25 26 27 28 29 30 31

November
1 2 3 4 5 6 7 8
9 10 11 12 13 14 15 16
17 18 19 20 21 22 23 24
25 26 27 28 29 30

December
1 2 3 4 5 6 7 8
9 10 11 12 13 14 15 16
17 18 19 20 21 22 23 24
25 26 27 28 29 30 31

2015

January
1 2 3 4 5 6 7 8
9 10 11 12 13 14 15 16
17 18 19 20 21 22 23 24
25 26 27 28 29 30 31

February
1 2 3 4 5 6 7 8
9 10 11 12 13 14 15 16
17 18 19 20 21 22 23 24
25 26 27 28

March
1 2 3 4 5 6 7 8
9 10 11 12 13 14 15 16
17 18 19 20 21 22 23 24
25 26 27 28 29 30 31

April
1 2 3 4 5 6 7 8
9 10 11 12 13 14 15 16
17 18 19 20 21 22 23 24
25 26 27 28 29 30

May
1 2 3 4 5 6 7 8
9 10 11 12 13 14 15 16
17 18 19 20 21 22 23 24
25 26 27 28 29 30 31

June
1 2 3 4 5 6 7 8
9 10 11 12 13 14 15 16
17 18 19 20 21 22 23 24
25 26 27 28 29 30

July
1 2 3 4 5 6 7 8
9 10 11 12 13 14 15 16
17 18 19 20 21 22 23 24
25 26 27 28 29 30 31

August
1 2 3 4 5 6 7 8
9 10 11 12 13 14 15 16
17 18 19 20 21 22 23 24
25 26 27 28 29 30 31

September
1 2 3 4 5 6 7 8
9 10 11 12 13 14 15 16
17 18 19 20 21 22 23 24
25 26 27 28 29 30

October
1 2 3 4 5 6 7 8
9 10 11 12 13 14 15 16
17 18 19 20 21 22 23 24
25 26 27 28 29 30 31

November
1 2 3 4 5 6 7 8
9 10 11 12 13 14 15 16
17 18 19 20 21 22 23 24
25 26 27 28 29 30

December
1 2 3 4 5 6 7 8
9 10 11 12 13 14 15 16
17 18 19 20 21 22 23 24
25 26 27 28 29 30 31

2016

January
1 2 3 4 5 6 7 8
9 10 11 12 13 14 15 16
17 18 19 20 21 22 23 24
25 26 27 28 29 30 31

February
1 2 3 4 5 6 7 8
9 10 11 12 13 14 15 16
17 18 19 20 21 22 23 24
25 26 27 28 29

March
1 2 3 4 5 6 7 8
9 10 11 12 13 14 15 16
17 18 19 20 21 22 23 24
25 26 27 28 29 30 31

April
1 2 3 4 5 6 7 8
9 10 11 12 13 14 15 16
17 18 19 20 21 22 23 24
25 26 27 28 29 30

May
1 2 3 4 5 6 7 8
9 10 11 12 13 14 15 16
17 18 19 20 21 22 23 24
25 26 27 28 29 30 31

June
1 2 3 4 5 6 7 8
9 10 11 12 13 14 15 16
17 18 19 20 21 22 23 24
25 26 27 28 29 30

July
1 2 3 4 5 6 7 8
9 10 11 12 13 14 15 16
17 18 19 20 21 22 23 24
25 26 27 28 29 30 31

August
1 2 3 4 5 6 7 8
9 10 11 12 13 14 15 16
17 18 19 20 21 22 23 24
25 26 27 28 29 30 31

September
1 2 3 4 5 6 7 8
9 10 11 12 13 14 15 16
17 18 19 20 21 22 23 24
25 26 27 28 29 30

October
1 2 3 4 5 6 7 8
9 10 11 12 13 14 15 16
17 18 19 20 21 22 23 24
25 26 27 28 29 30 31

November
1 2 3 4 5 6 7 8
9 10 11 12 13 14 15 16
17 18 19 20 21 22 23 24
25 26 27 28 29 30

December
1 2 3 4 5 6 7 8
9 10 11 12 13 14 15 16
17 18 19 20 21 22 23 24
25 26 27 28 29 30 31

2017

January
1 2 3 4 5 6 7 8
9 10 11 12 13 14 15 16
17 18 19 20 21 22 23 24
25 26 27 28 29 30 31

February
1 2 3 4 5 6 7 8
9 10 11 12 13 14 15 16
17 18 19 20 21 22 23 24
25 26 27 28

March
1 2 3 4 5 6 7 8
9 10 11 12 13 14 15 16
17 18 19 20 21 22 23 24
25 26 27 28 29 30 31

April
1 2 3 4 5 6 7 8
9 10 11 12 13 14 15 16
17 18 19 20 21 22 23 24
25 26 27 28 29 30

May
1 2 3 4 5 6 7 8
9 10 11 12 13 14 15 16
17 18 19 20 21 22 23 24
25 26 27 28 29 30 31

June
1 2 3 4 5 6 7 8
9 10 11 12 13 14 15 16
17 18 19 20 21 22 23 24
25 26 27 28 29 30

July
1 2 3 4 5 6 7 8
9 10 11 12 13 14 15 16
17 18 19 20 21 22 23 24
25 26 27 28 29 30 31

August
1 2 3 4 5 6 7 8
9 10 11 12 13 14 15 16
17 18 19 20 21 22 23 24
25 26 27 28 29 30 31

September
1 2 3 4 5 6 7 8
9 10 11 12 13 14 15 16
17 18 19 20 21 22 23 24
25 26 27 28 29 30

October
1 2 3 4 5 6 7 8
9 10 11 12 13 14 15 16
17 18 19 20 21 22 23 24
25 26 27 28 29 30 31

November
1 2 3 4 5 6 7 8
9 10 11 12 13 14 15 16
17 18 19 20 21 22 23 24
25 26 27 28 29 30

December
1 2 3 4 5 6 7 8
9 10 11 12 13 14 15 16
17 18 19 20 21 22 23 24
25 26 27 28 29 30 31

2018

January
1 2 3 4 5 6 7 8
9 10 11 12 13 14 15 16
17 18 19 20 21 22 23 24
25 26 27 28 29 30 31

February
1 2 3 4 5 6 7 8
9 10 11 12 13 14 15 16
17 18 19 20 21 22 23 24
25 26 27 28

March
1 2 3 4 5 6 7 8
9 10 11 12 13 14 15 16
17 18 19 20 21 22 23 24
25 26 27 28 29 30 31

April
1 2 3 4 5 6 7 8
9 10 11 12 13 14 15 16
17 18 19 20 21 22 23 24
25 26 27 28 29 30

May
1 2 3 4 5 6 7 8
9 10 11 12 13 14 15 16
17 18 19 20 21 22 23 24
25 26 27 28 29 30 31

June
1 2 3 4 5 6 7 8
9 10 11 12 13 14 15 16
17 18 19 20 21 22 23 24
25 26 27 28 29 30

July
1 2 3 4 5 6 7 8
9 10 11 12 13 14 15 16
17 18 19 20 21 22 23 24
25 26 27 28 29 30 31

August
1 2 3 4 5 6 7 8
9 10 11 12 13 14 15 16
17 18 19 20 21 22 23 24
25 26 27 28 29 30 31

September
1 2 3 4 5 6 7 8
9 10 11 12 13 14 15 16
17 18 19 20 21 22 23 24
25 26 27 28 29 30

October
1 2 3 4 5 6 7 8
9 10 11 12 13 14 15 16
17 18 19 20 21 22 23 24
25 26 27 28 29 30 31

November
1 2 3 4 5 6 7 8
9 10 11 12 13 14 15 16
17 18 19 20 21 22 23 24
25 26 27 28 29 30

December
1 2 3 4 5 6 7 8
9 10 11 12 13 14 15 16
17 18 19 20 21 22 23 24
25 26 27 28 29 30 31

2019

January
1 2 3 4 5 6 7 8
9 10 11 12 13 14 15 16
17 18 19 20 21 22 23 24
25 26 27 28 29 30 31

February
1 2 3 4 5 6 7 8
9 10 11 12 13 14 15 16
17 18 19 20 21 22 23 24
25 26 27 28

March
1 2 3 4 5 6 7 8
9 10 11 12 13 14 15 16
17 18 19 20 21 22 23 24
25 26 27 28 29 30 31

April
1 2 3 4 5 6 7 8
9 10 11 12 13 14 15 16
17 18 19 20 21 22 23 24
25 26 27 28 29 30

May
1 2 3 4 5 6 7 8
9 10 11 12 13 14 15 16
17 18 19 20 21 22 23 24
25 26 27 28 29 30 31

June
1 2 3 4 5 6 7 8
9 10 11 12 13 14 15 16
17 18 19 20 21 22 23 24
25 26 27 28 29 30

July
1 2 3 4 5 6 7 8
9 10 11 12 13 14 15 16
17 18 19 20 21 22 23 24
25 26 27 28 29 30 31

August
1 2 3 4 5 6 7 8
9 10 11 12 13 14 15 16
17 18 19 20 21 22 23 24
25 26 27 28 29 30 31

September
1 2 3 4 5 6 7 8
9 10 11 12 13 14 15 16
17 18 19 20 21 22 23 24
25 26 27 28 29 30

October
1 2 3 4 5 6 7 8
9 10 11 12 13 14 15 16
17 18 19 20 21 22 23 24
25 26 27 28 29 30 31

November
1 2 3 4 5 6 7 8
9 10 11 12 13 14 15 16
17 18 19 20 21 22 23 24
25 26 27 28 29 30

December
1 2 3 4 5 6 7 8
9 10 11 12 13 14 15 16
17 18 19 20 21 22 23 24
25 26 27 28 29 30 31

2020

January
1 2 3 4 5 6 7 8
9 10 11 12 13 14 15 16
17 18 19 20 21 22 23 24
25 26 27 28 29 30 31

February
1 2 3 4 5 6 7 8
9 10 11 12 13 14 15 16
17 18 19 20 21 22 23 24
25 26 27 28 29

March
1 2 3 4 5 6 7 8
9 10 11 12 13 14 15 16
17 18 19 20 21 22 23 24
25 26 27 28 29 30 31

April
1 2 3 4 5 6 7 8
9 10 11 12 13 14 15 16
17 18 19 20 21 22 23 24
25 26 27 28 29 30

May
1 2 3 4 5 6 7 8
9 10 11 12 13 14 15 16
17 18 19 20 21 22 23 24
25 26 27 28 29 30 31

June
1 2 3 4 5 6 7 8
9 10 11 12 13 14 15 16
17 18 19 20 21 22 23 24
25 26 27 28 29 30

July
1 2 3 4 5 6 7 8
9 10 11 12 13 14 15 16
17 18 19 20 21 22 23 24
25 26 27 28 29 30 31

August
1 2 3 4 5 6 7 8
9 10 11 12 13 14 15 16
17 18 19 20 21 22 23 24
25 26 27 28 29 30 31

September
1 2 3 4 5 6 7 8
9 10 11 12 13 14 15 16
17 18 19 20 21 22 23 24
25 26 27 28 29 30

October
1 2 3 4 5 6 7 8
9 10 11 12 13 14 15 16
17 18 19 20 21 22 23 24
25 26 27 28 29 30 31

November
1 2 3 4 5 6 7 8
9 10 11 12 13 14 15 16
17 18 19 20 21 22 23 24
25 26 27 28 29 30

December
1 2 3 4 5 6 7 8
9 10 11 12 13 14 15 16
17 18 19 20 21 22 23 24
25 26 27 28 29 30 31

2021

January
1 2 3 4 5 6 7 8
9 10 11 12 13 14 15 16
17 18 19 20 21 22 23 24
25 26 27 28 29 30 31

February
1 2 3 4 5 6 7 8
9 10 11 12 13 14 15 16
17 18 19 20 21 22 23 24
25 26 27 28

March
1 2 3 4 5 6 7 8
9 10 11 12 13 14 15 16
17 18 19 20 21 22 23 24
25 26 27 28 29 30 31

April
1 2 3 4 5 6 7 8
9 10 11 12 13 14 15 16
17 18 19 20 21 22 23 24
25 26 27 28 29 30

May
1 2 3 4 5 6 7 8
9 10 11 12 13 14 15 16
17 18 19 20 21 22 23 24
25 26 27 28 29 30 31

June
1 2 3 4 5 6 7 8
9 10 11 12 13 14 15 16
17 18 19 20 21 22 23 24
25 26 27 28 29 30

July
1 2 3 4 5 6 7 8
9 10 11 12 13 14 15 16
17 18 19 20 21 22 23 24
25 26 27 28 29 30 31

August
1 2 3 4 5 6 7 8
9 10 11 12 13 14 15 16
17 18 19 20 21 22 23 24
25 26 27 28 29 30 31

September
1 2 3 4 5 6 7 8
9 10 11 12 13 14 15 16
17 18 19 20 21 22 23 24
25 26 27 28 29 30

October
1 2 3 4 5 6 7 8
9 10 11 12 13 14 15 16
17 18 19 20 21 22 23 24
25 26 27 28 29 30 31

November
1 2 3 4 5 6 7 8
9 10 11 12 13 14 15 16
17 18 19 20 21 22 23 24
25 26 27 28 29 30

December
1 2 3 4 5 6 7 8
9 10 11 12 13 14 15 16
17 18 19 20 21 22 23 24
25 26 27 28 29 30 31

2022

January
1 2 3 4 5 6 7 8
9 10 11 12 13 14 15 16
17 18 19 20 21 22 23 24
25 26 27 28 29 30 31

February
1 2 3 4 5 6 7 8
9 10 11 12 13 14 15 16
17 18 19 20 21 22 23 24
25 26 27 28

March
1 2 3 4 5 6 7 8
9 10 11 12 13 14 15 16
17 18 19 20 21 22 23 24
25 26 27 28 29 30 31

April
1 2 3 4 5 6 7 8
9 10 11 12 13 14 15 16
17 18 19 20 21 22 23 24
25 26 27 28 29 30

May
1 2 3 4 5 6 7 8
9 10 11 12 13 14 15 16
17 18 19 20 21 22 23 24
25 26 27 28 29 30 31

June
1 2 3 4 5 6 7 8
9 10 11 12 13 14 15 16
17 18 19 20 21 22 23 24
25 26 27 28 29 30

July
1 2 3 4 5 6 7 8
9 10 11 12 13 14 15 16
17 18 19 20 21 22 23 24
25 26 27 28 29 30 31

August
1 2 3 4 5 6 7 8
9 10 11 12 13 14 15 16
17 18 19 20 21 22 23 24
25 26 27 28 29 30 31

September
1 2 3 4 5 6 7 8
9 10 11 12 13 14 15 16
17 18 19 20 21 22 23 24
25 26 27 28 29 30

October
1 2 3 4 5 6 7 8
9 10 11 12 13 14 15 16
17 18 19 20 21 22 23 24
25 26 27 28 29 30 31

November
1 2 3 4 5 6 7 8
9 10 11 12 13 14 15 16
17 18 19 20 21 22 23 24
25 26 27 28 29 30

December
1 2 3 4 5 6 7 8
9 10 11 12 13 14 15 16
17 18 19 20 21 22 23 24
25 26 27 28 29 30 31

2023

January
1 2 3 4 5 6 7 8
9 10 11 12 13 14 15 16
17 18 19 20 21 22 23 24
25 26 27 28 29 30 31

February
1 2 3 4 5 6 7 8
9 10 11 12 13 14 15 16
17 18 19 20 21 22 23 24
25 26 27 28

March
1 2 3 4 5 6 7 8
9 10 11 12 13 14 15 16
17 18 19 20 21 22 23 24
25 26 27 28 29 30 31

April
1 2 3 4 5 6 7 8
9 10 11 12 13 14 15 16
17 18 19 20 21 22 23 24
25 26 27 28 29 30

May
1 2 3 4 5 6 7 8
9 10 11 12 13 14 15 16
17 18 19 20 21 22 23 24
25 26 27 28 29 30 31

June
1 2 3 4 5 6 7 8
9 10 11 12 13 14 15 16
17 18 19 20 21 22 23 24
25 26 27 28 29 30

July
1 2 3 4 5 6 7 8
9 10 11 12 13 14 15 16
17 18 19 20 21 22 23 24
25 26 27 28 29 30 31

August
1 2 3 4 5 6 7 8
9 10 11 12 13 14 15 16
17 18 19 20 21 22 23 24
25 26 27 28 29 30 31

September
1 2 3 4 5 6 7 8
9 10 11 12 13 14 15 16
17 18 19 20 21 22 23 24
25 26 27 28 29 30

October
1 2 3 4 5 6 7 8
9 10 11 12 13 14 15 16
17 18 19 20 21 22 23 24
25 26 27 28 29 30 31

November
1 2 3 4 5 6 7 8
9 10 11 12 13 14 15 16
17 18 19 20 21 22 23 24
25 26 27 28 29 30

December
1 2 3 4 5 6 7 8
9 10 11 12 13 14 15 16
17 18 19 20 21 22 23 24
25 26 27 28 29 30 31

2024

January
1 2 3 4 5 6 7 8
9 10 11 12 13 14 15 16
17 18 19 20 21 22 23 24
25 26 27 28 29 30 31

February
1 2 3 4 5 6 7 8
9 10 11 12 13 14 15 16
17 18 19 20 21 22 23 24
25 26 27 28 29

March
1 2 3 4 5 6 7 8
9 10 11 12 13 14 15 16
17 18 19 20 21 22 23 24
25 26 27 28 29 30 31

April
1 2 3 4 5 6 7 8
9 10 11 12 13 14 15 16
17 18 19 20 21 22 23 24
25 26 27 28 29 30

May
1 2 3 4 5 6 7 8
9 10 11 12 13 14 15 16
17 18 19 20 21 22 23 24
25 26 27 28 29 30 31

June
1 2 3 4 5 6 7 8
9 10 11 12 13 14 15 16
17 18 19 20 21 22 23 24
25 26 27 28 29 30

July
1 2 3 4 5 6 7 8
9 10 11 12 13 14 15 16
17 18 19 20 21 22 23 24
25 26 27 28 29 30 31

August
1 2 3 4 5 6 7 8
9 10 11 12 13 14 15 16
17 18 19 20 21 22 23 24
25 26 27 28 29 30 31

September
1 2 3 4 5 6 7 8
9 10 11 12 13 14 15 16
17 18 19 20 21 22 23 24
25 26 27 28 29 30

October
1 2 3 4 5 6 7 8
9 10 11 12 13 14 15 16
17 18 19 20 21 22 23 24
25 26 27 28 29 30 31

November
1 2 3 4 5 6 7 8
9 10 11 12 13 14 15 16
17 18 19 20 21 22 23 24
25 26 27 28 29 30

December
1 2 3 4 5 6 7 8
9 10 11 12 13 14 15 16
17 18 19 20 21 22 23 24
25 26 27 28 29 30 31

2025

January
1 2 3 4 5 6 7 8
9 10 11 12 13 14 15 16
17 18 19 20 21 22 23 24
25 26 27 28 29 30 31

February
1 2 3 4 5 6 7 8
9 10 11 12 13 14 15 16
17 18 19 20 21 22 23 24
25 26 27 28

March
1 2 3 4 5 6 7 8
9 10 11 12 13 14 15 16
17 18 19 20 21 22 23 24
25 26 27 28 29 30 31

April
1 2 3 4 5 6 7 8
9 10 11 12 13 14 15 16
17 18 19 20 21 22 23 24
25 26 27 28 29 30

May
1 2 3 4 5 6 7 8
9 10 11 12 13 14 15 16
17 18 19 20 21 22 23 24
25 26 27 28 29 30 31

June
1 2 3 4 5 6 7 8
9 10 11 12 13 14 15 16
17 18 19 20 21 22 23 24
25 26 27 28 29 30

July
1 2 3 4 5 6 7 8
9 10 11 12 13 14 15 16
17 18 19 20 21 22 23 24
25 26 27 28 29 30 31

August
1 2 3 4 5 6 7 8
9 10 11 12 13 14 15 16
17 18 19 20 21 22 23 24
25 26 27 28 29 30 31

September
1 2 3 4 5 6 7 8
9 10 11 12 13 14 15 16
17 18 19 20 21 22 23 24
25 26 27 28 29 30

October
1 2 3 4 5 6 7 8
9 10 11 12 13 14 15 16
17 18 19 20 21 22 23 24
25 26 27 28 29 30 31

November
1 2 3 4 5 6 7 8
9 10 11 12 13 14 15 16
17 18 19 20 21 22 23 24
25 26 27 28 29 30

December
1 2 3 4 5 6 7 8
9 10 11 12 13 14 15 16
17 18 19 20 21 22 23 24
25 26 27 28 29 30 31

2026

January
1 2 3 4 5 6 7 8
9 10 11 12 13 14 15 16
17 18 19 20 21 22 23 24
25 26 27 28 29 30 31

February
1 2 3 4 5 6 7 8
9 10 11 12 13 14 15 16
17 18 19 20 21 22 23 24
25 26 27 28

March
1 2 3 4 5 6 7 8
9 10 11 12 13 14 15 16
17 18 19 20 21 22 23 24
25 26 27 28 29 30 31

April
1 2 3 4 5 6 7 8
9 10 11 12 13 14 15 16
17 18 19 20 21 22 23 24
25 26 27 28 29 30

May
1 2 3 4 5 6 7 8
9 10 11 12 13 14 15 16
17 18 19 20 21 22 23 24
25 26 27 28 29 30 31

June
1 2 3 4 5 6 7 8
9 10 11 12 13 14 15 16
17 18 19 20 21 22 23 24
25 26 27 28 29 30

July
1 2 3 4 5 6 7 8
9 10 11 12 13 14 15 16
17 18 19 20 21 22 23 24
25 26 27 28 29 30 31

August
1 2 3 4 5 6 7 8
9 10 11 12 13 14 15 16
17 18 19 20 21 22 23 24
25 26 27 28 29 30 31

September
1 2 3 4 5 6 7 8
9 10 11 12 13 14 15 16
17 18 19 20 21 22 23 24
25 26 27 28 29 30

October
1 2 3 4 5 6 7 8
9 10 11 12 13 14 15 16
17 18 19 20 21 22 23 24
25 26 27 28 29 30 31

November
1 2 3 4 5 6 7 8
9 10 11 12 13 14 15 16
17 18 19 20 21 22 23 24
25 26 27 28 29 30

December
1 2 3 4 5 6 7 8
9 10 11 12 13 14 15 16
17 18 19 20 21 22 23 24
25 26 27 28 29 30 31

2027

January
1 2 3 4 5 6 7 8
9 10 11 12 13 14 15 16
17 18 19 20 21 22 23 24
25 26 27 28 29 30 31

February
1 2 3 4 5 6 7 8
9 10 11 12 13 14 15 16
17 18 19 20 21 22 23 24
25 26 27 28

March
1 2 3 4 5 6 7 8
9 10 11 12 13 14 15 16
17 18 19 20 21 22 23 24
25 26 27 28 29 30 31

April
1 2 3 4 5 6 7 8
9 10 11 12 13 14 15 16
17 18 19 20 21 22 23 24
25 26 27 28 29 30

May
1 2 3 4 5 6 7 8
9 10 11 12 13 14 15 16
17 18 19 20 21 22 23 24
25 26 27 28 29 30 31

June
1 2 3 4 5 6 7 8
9 10 11 12 13 14 15 16
17 18 19 20 21 22 23 24
25 26 27 28 29 30

July
1 2 3 4 5 6 7 8
9 10 11 12 13 14 15 16
17 18 19 20 21 22 23 24
25 26 27 28 29 30 31

August
1 2 3 4 5 6 7 8
9 10 11 12 13 14 15 16
17 18 19 20 21 22 23 24
25 26 27 28 29 30 31

September
1 2 3 4 5 6 7 8
9 10 11 12 13 14 15 16
17 18 19 20 21 22 23 24
25 26 27 28 29 30

October
1 2 3 4 5 6 7 8
9 10 11 12 13 14 15 16
17 18 19 20 21 22 23 24
25 26 27 28 29 30 31

November
1 2 3 4 5 6 7 8
9 10 11 12 13 14 15 16
17 18 19 20 21 22 23 24
25 26 27 28 29 30

December
1 2 3 4 5 6 7 8
9 10 11 12 13 14 15 16
17 18 19 20 21 22 23 24
25 26 27 28 29 30 31

2028

January
1 2 3 4 5 6 7 8
9 10 11 12 13 14 15 16
17 18 19 20 21 22 23 24
25 26 27 28 29 30 31

February
1 2 3 4 5 6 7 8
9 10 11 12 13 14 15 16
17 18 19 20 21 22 23 24
25 26 27 28 29

March
1 2 3 4 5 6 7 8
9 10 11 12 13 14 15 16
17 18 19 20 21 22 23 24
25 26 27 28 29 30 31

April
1 2 3 4 5 6 7 8
9 10 11 12 13 14 15 16
17 18 19 20 21 22 23 24
25 26 27 28 29 30

May
1 2 3 4 5 6 7 8
9 10 11 12 13 14 15 16
17 18 19 20 21 22 23 24
25 26 27 28 29 30 31

June
1 2 3 4 5 6 7 8
9 10 11 12 13 14 15 16
17 18 19 20 21 22 23 24
25 26 27 28 29 30

July
1 2 3 4 5 6 7 8
9 10 11 12 13 14 15 16
17 18 19 20 21 22 23 24
25 26 27 28 29 30 31

August
1 2 3 4 5 6 7 8
9 10 11 12 13 14 15 16
17 18 19 20 21 22 23 24
25 26 27 28 29 30 31

September
1 2 3 4 5 6 7 8
9 10 11 12 13 14 15 16
17 18 19 20 21 22 23 24
25 26 27 28 29 30

October
1 2 3 4 5 6 7 8
9 10 11 12 13 14 15 16
17 18 19 20 21 22 23 24
25 26 27 28 29 30 31

November
1 2 3 4 5 6 7 8
9 10 11 12 13 14 15 16
17 18 19 20 21 22 23 24
25 26 27 28 29 30

December
1 2 3 4 5 6 7 8
9 10 11 12 13 14 15 16
17 18 19 20 21 22 23 24
25 26 27 28 29 30 31

2029

January
1 2 3 4 5 6 7 8
9 10 11 12 13 14 15 16
17 18 19 20 21 22 23 24
25 26 27 28 29 30 31

February
1 2 3 4 5 6 7 8
9 10 11 12 13 14 15 16
17 18 19 20 21 22 23 24
25 26 27 28

March
1 2 3 4 5 6 7 8
9 10 11 12 13 14 15 16
17 18 19 20 21 22 23 24
25 26 27 28 29 30 31

April
1 2 3 4 5 6 7 8
9 10 11 12 13 14 15 16
17 18 19 20 21 22 23 24
25 26 27 28 29 30

May
1 2 3 4 5 6 7 8
9 10 11 12 13 14 15 16
17 18 19 20 21 22 23 24
25 26 27 28 29 30 31

June
1 2 3 4 5 6 7 8
9 10 11 12 13 14 15 16
17 18 19 20 21 22 23 24
25 26 27 28 29 30

July
1 2 3 4 5 6 7 8
9 10 11 12 13 14 15 16
17 18 19 20 21 22 23 24
25 26 27 28 29 30 31

August
1 2 3 4 5 6 7 8
9 10 11 12 13 14 15 16
17 18 19 20 21 22 23 24
25 26 27 28 29 30 31

September
1 2 3 4 5 6 7 8
9 10 11 12 13 14 15 16
17 18 19 20 21 22 23 24
25 26 27 28 29 30

October
1 2 3 4 5 6 7 8
9 10 11 12 13 14 15 16
17 18 19 20 21 22 23 24
25 26 27 28 29 30 31

November
1 2 3 4 5 6 7 8
9 10 11 12 13 14 15 16
17 18 19 20 21 22 23 24
25 26 27 28 29 30

December
1 2 3 4 5 6 7 8
9 10 11 12 13 14 15 16
17 18 19 20 21 22 23 24
25 26 27 28 29 30 31

2030

January
1 2 3 4 5 6 7 8
9 10 11 12 13 14 15 16
17 18 19 20 21 22 23 24
25 26 27 28 29 30 31

February
1 2 3 4 5 6 7 8
9 10 11 12 13 14 15 16
17 18 19 20 21 22 23 24
25 26 27 28

March
1 2 3 4 5 6 7 8
9 10 11 12 13 14 15 16
17 18 19 20 21 22 23 24
25 26 27 28 29 30 31

April
1 2 3 4 5 6 7 8
9 10 11 12 13 14 15 16
17 18 19 20 21 22 23 24
25 26 27 28 29 30

May
1 2 3 4 5 6 7 8
9 10 11 12 13 14 15 16
17 18 19 20 21 22 23 24
25 26 27 28 29 30 31

June
1 2 3 4 5 6 7 8
9 10 11 12 13 14 15 16
17 18 19 20 21 22 23 24
25 26 27 28 29 30

July
1 2 3 4 5 6 7 8
9 10 11 12 13 14 15 16
17 18 19 20 21 22 23 24
25 26 27 28 29 30 31

August
1 2 3 4 5 6 7 8
9 10 11 12 13 14 15 16
17 18 19 20 21 22 23 24
25 26 27 28 29 30 31

September
1 2 3 4 5 6 7 8
9 10 11 12 13 14 15 16
17 18 19 20 21 22 23 24
25 26 27 28 29 30

October
1 2 3 4 5 6 7 8
9 10 11 12 13 14 15 16
17 18 19 20 21 22 23 24
25 26 27 28 29 30 31

November
1 2 3 4 5 6 7 8
9 10 11 12 13 14 15 16
17 18 19 20 21 22 23 24
25 26 27 28 29 30

December
1 2 3 4 5 6 7 8
9 10 11 12 13 14 15 16
17 18 19 20 21 22 23 24
25 26 27 28 29 30 31

2031

January
1 2 3 4 5 6 7 8
9 10 11 12 13 14 15 16
17 18 19 20 21 22 23 24
25 26 27 28 29 30 31

February
1 2 3 4 5 6 7 8
9 10 11 12 13 14 15 16
17 18 19 20 21 22 23 24
25 26 27 28

March
1 2 3 4 5 6 7 8
9 10 11 12 13 14 15 16
17 18 19 20 21 22 23 24
25 26 27 28 29 30 31

April
1 2 3 4 5 6 7 8
9 10 11 12 13 14 15 16
17 18 19 20 21 22 23 24
25 26 27 28 29 30

May
1 2 3 4 5 6 7 8
9 10 11 12 13 14 15 16
17 18 19 20 21 22 23 24
25 26 27 28 29 30 31

June
1 2 3 4 5 6 7 8
9 10 11 12 13 14 15 16
17 18 19 20 21 22 23 24
25 26 27 28 29 30

July
1 2 3 4 5 6 7 8
9 10 11 12 13 14 15 16
17 18 19 20 21 22 23 24
25 26 27 28 29 30 31

August
1 2 3 4 5 6 7 8
9 10 11 12 13 14 15 16
17 18 19 20 21 22 23 24
25 26 27 28 29 30 31

September
1 2 3 4 5 6 7 8
9 10 11 12 13 14 15 16
17 18 19 20 21 22 23 24
25 26 27 28 29 30

October
1 2 3 4 5 6 7 8
9 10 11 12 13 14 15 16
17 18 19 20 21 22 23 24
25 26 27 28 29 30 31

November
1 2 3 4 5 6 7 8
9 10 11 12 13 14 15 16
17 18 19 20 21 22 23 24
25 26 27 28 29 30

December
1 2 3 4 5 6 7 8
9 10 11 12 13 14 15 16
17 18 19 20 21 22 23 24
25 26 27 28 29 30 31

2032

January
1 2 3 4 5 6 7 8
9 10 11 12 13 14 15 16
17 18 19 20 21 22 23 24
25 26 27 28 29 30 31

February
1 2 3 4 5 6 7 8
9 10 11 12 13 14 15 16
17 18 19 20 21 22 23 24
25 26 27 28 29

March
1 2 3 4 5 6 7 8
9 10 11 12 13 14 15 16
17 18 19 20 21 22 23 24
25 26 27 28 29 30 31

April
1 2 3 4 5 6 7 8
9 10 11 12 13 14 15 16
17 18 19 20 21 22 23 24
25 26 27 28 29 30

May
1 2 3 4 5 6 7 8
9 10 11 12 13 14 15 16
17 18 19 20 21 22 23 24
25 26 27 28 29 30 31

June
1 2 3 4 5 6 7 8
9 10 11 12 13 14 15 16
17 18 19 20 21 22 23 24
25 26 27 28 29 30

July
1 2 3 4 5 6 7 8
9 10 11 12 13 14 15 16
17 18 19 20 21 22 23 24
25 26 27 28 29 30 31

August
1 2 3 4 5 6 7 8
9 10 11 12 13 14 15 16
17 18 19 20 21 22 23 24
25 26 27 28 29 30 31

September
1 2 3 4 5 6 7 8
9 10 11 12 13 14 15 16
17 18 19 20 21 22 23 24
25 26 27 28 29 30

October
1 2 3 4 5 6 7 8
9 10 11 12 13 14 15 16
17 18 19 20 21 22 23 24
25 26 27 28 29 30 31

November
1 2 3 4 5 6 7 8
9 10 11 12 13 14 15 16
17 18 19 20 21 22 23 24
25 26 27 28 29 30

December
1 2 3 4 5 6 7 8
9 10 11 12 13 14 15 16
17 18 19 20 21 22 23 24
25 26 27 28 29 30 31

2033

January
1 2 3 4 5 6 7 8
9 10 11 12 13 14 15 16
17 18 19 20 21 22 23 24
25 26 27 28 29 30 31

February
1 2 3 4 5 6 7 8
9 10 11 12 13 14 15 16
17 18 19 20 21 22 23 24
25 26 27 28

March
1 2 3 4 5 6 7 8
9 10 11 12 13 14 15 16
17 18 19 20 21 22 23 24
25 26 27 28 29 30 31

April
1 2 3 4 5 6 7 8
9 10 11 12 13 14 15 16
17 18 19 20 21 22 23 24
25 26 27 28 29 30

May
1 2 3 4 5 6 7 8
9 10 11 12 13 14 15 16
17 18 19 20 21 22 23 24
25 26 27 28 29 30 31

June
1 2 3 4 5 6 7 8
9 10 11 12 13 14 15 16
17 18 19 20 21 22 23 24
25 26 27 28 29 30

July
1 2 3 4 5 6 7 8
9 10 11 12 13 14 15 16
17 18 19 20 21 22 23 24
25 26 27 28 29 30 31

August
1 2 3 4 5 6 7 8
9 10 11 12 13 14 15 16
17 18 19 20 21 22 23 24
25 26 27 28 29 30 31

September
1 2 3 4 5 6 7 8
9 10 11 12 13 14 15 16
17 18 19 20 21 22 23 24
25 26 27 28 29 30

October
1 2 3 4 5 6 7 8
9 10 11 12 13 14 15 16
17 18 19 20 21 22 23 24
25 26 27 28 29 30 31

November
1 2 3 4 5 6 7 8
9 10 11 12 13 14 15 16
17 18 19 20 21 22 23 24
25 26 27 28 29 30

December
1 2 3 4 5 6 7 8
9 10 11 12 13 14 15 16
17 18 19 20 21 22 23 24
25 26 27 28 29 30 31

2034

January
1 2 3 4 5 6 7 8
9 10 11 12 13 14 15 16
17 18 19 20 21 22 23 24
25 26 27 28 29 30 31

February
1 2 3 4 5 6 7 8
9 10 11 12 13 14 15 16
17 18 19 20 21 22 23 24
25 26 27 28

March
1 2 3 4 5 6 7 8
9 10 11 12 13 14 15 16
17 18 19 20 21 22 23 24
25 26 27 28 29 30 31

April
1 2 3 4 5 6 7 8
9 10 11 12 13 14 15 16
17 18 19 20 21 22 23 24
25 26 27 28 29 30

May
1 2 3 4 5 6 7 8
9 10 11 12 13 14 15 16
17 18 19 20 21 22 23 24
25 26 27 28 29 30 31

June
1 2 3 4 5 6 7 8
9 10 11 12 13 14 15 16
17 18 19 20 21 22 23 24
25 26 27 28 29 30

July
1 2 3 4 5 6 7 8
9 10 11 12 13 14 15 16
17 18 19 20 21 22 23 24
25 26 27 28 29 30 31

August
1 2 3 4 5 6 7 8
9 10 11 12 13 14 15 16
17 18 19 20 21 22 23 24
25 26 27 28 29 30 31

September
1 2 3 4 5 6 7 8
9 10 11 12 13 14 15 16
17 18 19 20 21 22 23 24
25 26 27 28 29 30

October
1 2 3 4 5 6 7 8
9 10 11 12 13 14 15 16
17 18 19 20 21 22 23 24
25 26 27 28 29 30 31

November
1 2 3 4 5 6 7 8
9 10 11 12 13 14 15 16
17 18 19 20 21 22 23 24
25 26 27 28 29 30

December
1 2 3 4 5 6 7 8
9 10 11 12 13 14 15 16
17 18 19 20 21 22 23 24
25 26 27 28 29 30 31

Story of your life

You are obviously the most interesting chapter of their life, but what did your partner do before meeting you? To understand them, you must understand their past. Describe what you know of their life before you in detail here, and check with them for accuracy and libel.

Before he had the good luck to cross my path,

Checklist of essential topics to cover: Birth ☐ Childhood ☐ Family ☐ Schooling ☐ Teenage crushes ☐ Teenage crises ☐ Travels ☐ Ambitions ☐

Before she was fortunate enough to meet me,

Checklist of essential topics to cover: Birth □ Childhood □ Family □ Schooling □ Teenage crushes □ Teenage crises □ Travels □ Ambitions □

Intimacy test

By this relatively advanced stage in your relationship, you should be aware of the smallest details of your lover's everyday existence. Take this simple test to confirm your status as the world's foremost expert on him or her.

Her

Date of birth............./............./............./

Place of birth...

Brand of toothbrush..

Brand of toothpaste...

Brand of soap..

Brand of shampoo..

Brand of conditioner...

Brand of beer...

Brand of cola...

Brand of milk...

Brand of yoghurt..

Brand of cereal..

Brand of coffee..

Brand of ice cream...

Brand of spirits..

Brand of tampon...

Brand of bottled water..

Brand of toilet paper...

Brand of deodorant...

Brand of make-up...

Brand of watch...

Brand of camera...

Brand of chewing gum..

Date of birth............/............/............/

Place of birth..

Brand of toothbrush...

Brand of toothpaste..

Brand of soap..

Brand of shampoo..

Brand of conditioner..

Brand of beer..

Brand of cola..

Brand of milk..

Brand of yoghurt..

Brand of cereal..

Brand of coffee..

Brand of ice cream..

Brand of spirits..

Brand of condom..

Brand of bottled water..

Brand of toilet paper..

Brand of deodorant..

Brand of razor blades..

Brand of watch..

Brand of camera..

Brand of chewing gum..

Map of your heart

Words alone cannot do justice to the delphic intricacy of your personalities. Follow the example below and try to delineate each other's hearts. Use a pencil though, as you may need several attempts to represent them accurately.

Example

BROKEN AREA

DEAD BIT
(Divorce litigation)

BOB
(first love)

LOVE OF MY LIFE

Mr.......... John

Higgins

CHOCOLATE

KITTENS

BABIES

SELF LOVE

DARK CORNER
(KEEP OUT)

Likes & dislikes

After a lifetime spent together, your personalities should eventually meld into one, with the same views, memories and tastes. Hasten that happy outcome by keeping track of the things the two of you both love or hate.

Item	We like	We dislike	We differ*
Broccoli	✓		
Cycling			
Marmalade			✓
Space travel	✓		
Horror films		✓	
John Lennon	✓		
Botticelli		✓	
Guns		✓	
Naturism			
Black holes	✓		
Effort	✓		
Pedal bins			
Mice		✓	
Greek	✓		
Shellfish	✓		
Communism		✓	
Dawn			✓
Napoleon		✓	
Parachutes	✓		
Chaos			✓
Hypnotists	✓		
Babies	✓		
Wine	✓		
Spaniards	✓		
Traffic lights		✓	
Gossip			✓
Famine		✓	
Baguettes	✓		
Full frontal nudity	✓		
Social democracy	✓		
Sweet	✓		
Sour	✓		
Iniquity			
Freckles			✓
Barcodes			
Anarchy		✓	
Eating out	✓		
Bottled water	✓		
Modern art	✓		
Rap	✓		
Plastic			✓
Apple pie			✓
Budapest			
Baywatch			
Scrambled eggs	✓		
Nanotechnology	✓		

Item	We like	We dislike	We differ
Basketball			✓
Coke			✓
Pepsi			✓
Mirrors	✓		
Purple			✓
Terrorism		✓	
Camping	✓		
Beards	✓		
Saturn	✓		
Civil rights	✓		
Market research	✓		
Dominos	✓		
Rhododendrons			
Supergirl	✓		
Cufflinks	✓		
Showers	✓		
Fire	✓		
Tequila			✓
Earthquakes	✓		
Headphones			
Dinner parties	✓		
Soup			✓
Primordial soup			
Whistling	✓		
Grammar			✓
Nightmares		✓	
Ballistic missiles		✓	
Suspenders			
Poetry			
Arthritis		✓	
Dolly Parton			✓
Advertising	✓		
Hot dogs	✓		
Proust			
Balaclavas	✓		
Thunderstorms	✓		
Airports	✓		
Indecision		✓	
Deuteronomy			
Toast	✓		
Mildew			✓
Spanking	✓		
Consensus			
Marble			✓
California	✓		
Astronauts	✓		

Item	We like	We dislike	We differ
Tagliatelle	✓		
Cocaine			✓
Ironing		✓	
Jumble sales			
Strangers			✓
Biceps	✓		
Trigonometry		✓	
House sitting			
Free markets			
Salvation			
Paperclips	✓		
Orgasms	✓		
Sand		✓	
Blazers	✓		
Supersize meals			✓
Black magic			
Gerbils		✓	
Remixes	✓		
Salami			✓
Betamax			
Prehistory			
Bill Gates	✓		
Spring	✓		
Business cards	✓		
Round pegs	✓		
Square holes		✓	
Breakdancing	✓		
Spontaneity	✓		
Calculators	✓		
Fax machines	✓		
Hope			
Tasmania	✓		
Stripes	✓		
Viagra		✓	
Caravaggio			
Stupidity		✓	
Nelson Mandela	✓		
Ballrooms			✓
Recycling	✓		
Coconuts	✓		
Mascara			✓
Milkshakes			✓
Plywood			✓
Tuesdays	✓		
Running	✓		
Aircraft carriers			

Item	We like	We dislike	We differ
Mimes		✓	
Beauty	✓		
Shadows		✓	
Culture	✓		
Shower gel			✓
Chainsaws		✓	
Alopecia		✓	
Timidity	✓		
Plasticine		✓	
Cantilevering			
Taboos			
Menhirs			
Song	✓		
Suicide		✓	
Chopsticks	✓		
Spirals	✓		
Tamagotchis			✓
Instamatics		✓	
Catalogues	✓		
Exits			✓
Ciphers			
Witchcraft		✓	
Catamites			
Asphalt	✓		
Dna	✓		
Rock'n'roll	✓		
Ecuadoreans			
Photosynthesis	✓		
Leprosy			
Satellites			
Monkfish			
Tasmania	✓		
Repetition			
Gimmicks			
Hurricanes			
Trimesters			
Carnivals			
Self-plagiarism			
Belly laughter			
Zorro			
Doughnuts			
War			
Peace			
Christmas			
Minneapolis			
Spatulas			

Item	We like	We dislike	We differ
Gorgonzola			
Poker			
Arranged marriages			
Conifers			
Freak shows			
Punctuality			
Sweepstakes			
Absent-mindedness			
Rainbows			
Needles			
Tijuana			
Moon's dark side			
Reptiles			
Appendicitis			
Seabass			
Traffic			
Imperialism			
Soap operas			
Golden girls			
Tetris			
Archaeology			
Deadlines			
Spam			
Lithium batteries			
Lithium			
Zombies			
Meg Ryan			
Paraguay			
Insecticide			
Revolution			
Radio personalities			
Forks			
Watercoolers			
Eclipses			
Federalism			
Blondes			
Synonyms			
Jonas Jansson			
Martyrdom			
Elephants			
Sodomy			
Miracles			
Bacon			
Big Ben			
Mistakes			
Outspokenness			

Haikus	☐	☐	☐	Achievement	☐	☐	☐	Bluffing	☐	☐	☐	Mercenaries	☐	☐	☐	Dolce vita	☐	☐	☐
Snowploughs	☐	☐	☐	Sneakers	☐	☐	☐	Sushi	☐	☐	☐	Cats	☐	☐	☐	Interest rates	☐	☐	☐
Pasta	☐	☐	☐	Regrets	☐	☐	☐	Marigolds	☐	☐	☐	Dogs	☐	☐	☐	Ladders	☐	☐	☐
Drumsticks	☐	☐	☐	Speeding	☐	☐	☐	Propaganda	☐	☐	☐	Getting lost	☐	☐	☐	Panna cotta	☐	☐	☐
Matching socks	☐	☐	☐	Hatching plots	☐	☐	☐	Rollercoasters	☐	☐	☐	Neighbours	☐	☐	☐	Sex	☐	☐	☐
Liszt	☐	☐	☐	Agatha Christie	☐	☐	☐	Einstein	☐	☐	☐	Prozac	☐	☐	☐	Desert islands	☐	☐	☐
Lobster	☐	☐	☐	Opium	☐	☐	☐	Newton	☐	☐	☐	Bob Dylan	☐	☐	☐	Museums	☐	☐	☐
Dreams come true	☐	☐	☐	Merchandizing	☐	☐	☐	Hawking	☐	☐	☐	Forests	☐	☐	☐	Irony	☐	☐	☐
Tanks	☐	☐	☐	Fifth Avenue	☐	☐	☐	Kleptomania	☐	☐	☐	Sycophants	☐	☐	☐	Radioactivity	☐	☐	☐
Horoscopes	☐	☐	☐	Peace and quiet	☐	☐	☐	Reruns	☐	☐	☐	Helicopters	☐	☐	☐	Milk	☐	☐	☐
Patriotism	☐	☐	☐	Crooning	☐	☐	☐	Ice cream	☐	☐	☐	Benrik	☐	☐	☐	Casablanca	☐	☐	☐
Impressionism	☐	☐	☐	Big business	☐	☐	☐	Punctuation	☐	☐	☐	Spare ribs	☐	☐	☐	Funerals	☐	☐	☐
Raspberries	☐	☐	☐	Hollywood	☐	☐	☐	Judo	☐	☐	☐	Lego	☐	☐	☐	Woody Allen	☐	☐	☐
Elegance	☐	☐	☐	Prudence	☐	☐	☐	Life on the edge	☐	☐	☐	Mount Everest	☐	☐	☐	Danger	☐	☐	☐
Star Wars	☐	☐	☐	Halogen lamps	☐	☐	☐	Cigars	☐	☐	☐	Migraines	☐	☐	☐	Hair bands	☐	☐	☐
Bourgeois guilt	☐	☐	☐	Golf	☐	☐	☐	Mozzarella	☐	☐	☐	Libraries	☐	☐	☐	Conferences	☐	☐	☐
Hinges	☐	☐	☐	Fascism	☐	☐	☐	Destitution	☐	☐	☐	Blushing	☐	☐	☐	Hyenas	☐	☐	☐
Olympic games	☐	☐	☐	Garlic bread	☐	☐	☐	Atari	☐	☐	☐	Fast food	☐	☐	☐	Exercise	☐	☐	☐
Cardigans	☐	☐	☐	Picasso	☐	☐	☐	Swearing	☐	☐	☐	Marlon Brando	☐	☐	☐	Plutocracy	☐	☐	☐
Lawyers	☐	☐	☐	Travel	☐	☐	☐	Mass murder	☐	☐	☐	Nazism	☐	☐	☐	Porcini	☐	☐	☐
Onion soup	☐	☐	☐	Weirdness	☐	☐	☐	Parking	☐	☐	☐	Champagne	☐	☐	☐	Handshakes	☐	☐	☐
Weeding	☐	☐	☐	Slamming doors	☐	☐	☐	Brad Pitt	☐	☐	☐	Flower arranging	☐	☐	☐	Oxygen	☐	☐	☐
Abraham Lincoln	☐	☐	☐	Sharks	☐	☐	☐	Self-help books	☐	☐	☐	Bakeries	☐	☐	☐	Motherhood	☐	☐	☐
Mystery	☐	☐	☐	Architects	☐	☐	☐	Electricity	☐	☐	☐	Political debate	☐	☐	☐	Smurfs	☐	☐	☐
Custard	☐	☐	☐	School	☐	☐	☐	Speeches	☐	☐	☐	Fresh air	☐	☐	☐	Satin	☐	☐	☐
Bugs Bunny	☐	☐	☐	Utopia	☐	☐	☐	Pride	☐	☐	☐	New shoes	☐	☐	☐	Hot chocolate	☐	☐	☐
Ebola	☐	☐	☐	Sad songs	☐	☐	☐	Prejudice	☐	☐	☐	Jingles	☐	☐	☐	Fate	☐	☐	☐
Mischief	☐	☐	☐	Flight simulators	☐	☐	☐	Hit parades	☐	☐	☐	Trainspotting	☐	☐	☐	Dinosaurs	☐	☐	☐
Segways	☐	☐	☐	Popcorn	☐	☐	☐	Weather girls	☐	☐	☐	Small talk	☐	☐	☐	Emotional trauma	☐	☐	☐
France	☐	☐	☐	Camels	☐	☐	☐	Mustard	☐	☐	☐	Egg fried rice	☐	☐	☐	Vogue	☐	☐	☐
Astigmatism	☐	☐	☐	3B pencils	☐	☐	☐	French mustard	☐	☐	☐	Sunlight	☐	☐	☐	Bill Clinton	☐	☐	☐
Solar power	☐	☐	☐	Gravity	☐	☐	☐	Piano concertos	☐	☐	☐	Cunning plans	☐	☐	☐	Daydreaming	☐	☐	☐
Penguins	☐	☐	☐	Innuendo	☐	☐	☐	Brutality	☐	☐	☐	Jack Daniels	☐	☐	☐	Confrontation	☐	☐	☐
Air fresheners	☐	☐	☐	Money	☐	☐	☐	Stifled yawns	☐	☐	☐	Game shows	☐	☐	☐	Spinach	☐	☐	☐
Masturbation	☐	☐	☐	Brilliance	☐	☐	☐	Symmetry	☐	☐	☐	Ducks	☐	☐	☐	Unemployment	☐	☐	☐
Jazz	☐	☐	☐	Ghettos	☐	☐	☐	Gherkins	☐	☐	☐	Ice buckets	☐	☐	☐	Croissants	☐	☐	☐
Roadworks	☐	☐	☐	Plan Bs	☐	☐	☐	Compilations	☐	☐	☐	Competence	☐	☐	☐	Pop art	☐	☐	☐
Autumn leaves	☐	☐	☐	Motion sickness	☐	☐	☐	Disney	☐	☐	☐	Waterbeds	☐	☐	☐	Silicon valley	☐	☐	☐
Religion	☐	☐	☐	Lunar landings	☐	☐	☐	Bad news	☐	☐	☐	Gardening	☐	☐	☐	Futility	☐	☐	☐
Esperanto	☐	☐	☐	Tattoos	☐	☐	☐	Shakespeare	☐	☐	☐	Sex in the city	☐	☐	☐	Bearnaise sauce	☐	☐	☐
Sangria	☐	☐	☐	Base jumping	☐	☐	☐	Simpletons	☐	☐	☐	Prawns	☐	☐	☐	Frankincense	☐	☐	☐
Logos	☐	☐	☐	Bellinis	☐	☐	☐	Mercy	☐	☐	☐	Imitation	☐	☐	☐	Myrrh	☐	☐	☐
Fingerprints	☐	☐	☐	Violence	☐	☐	☐	Explosions	☐	☐	☐	Flattery	☐	☐	☐	Key rings	☐	☐	☐
Molotov cocktails	☐	☐	☐	Teddy bears	☐	☐	☐	Surprises	☐	☐	☐	Sincerity	☐	☐	☐	Philosophy	☐	☐	☐
Strudel	☐	☐	☐	Hallucinations	☐	☐	☐	Subtlety	☐	☐	☐	Niagara Falls	☐	☐	☐	Sesame street	☐	☐	☐
Scandal	☐	☐	☐	Pimples	☐	☐	☐	Carpet	☐	☐	☐	Buzzers	☐	☐	☐	Each other	☐	☐	☐

Would you still love me if...

In theory, you should love everything about the other, even their faults. In practice, the strongest love has its limits. Leaving the toilet seat up may be excusable, but war crimes, perhaps, are not. Use these pages to set the boundaries of your tolerance.

Would you still love me if I...

Voted Communist	Went bald	Had a sex change	Became the new face of thrush prevention	Joined the hare-krishna
Yes ☐ No ☐	Yes ☐ No ☐	Yes ☐ No ☐	Yes ☐ No ☐	Yes ☐ No ☐
Inherited an arms dealership	Sold out to the mass market	Became a crossword fanatic	Campaigned for the return of slavery	Adopted a donkey
Yes ☐ No ☐	Yes ☐ No ☐	Yes ☐ No ☐	Yes ☐ No ☐	Yes ☐ No ☐
Gatecrashed the palace	Imploded	Sought political asylum	Sold my body on the streets	Changed back into a frog
Yes ☐ No ☐	Yes ☐ No ☐	Yes ☐ No ☐	Yes ☐ No ☐	Yes ☐ No ☐
Wrote a book about us	Managed a brothel	Insulted your grandmother	Didn't flush	Was secretly related to you
Yes ☐ No ☐	Yes ☐ No ☐	Yes ☐ No ☐	Yes ☐ No ☐	Yes ☐ No ☐
Discovered I was related to Hitler	Slept with your lookalike by mistake	Volunteered for a dangerous mission	Wore fur	Had a glass eye
Yes ☐ No ☐	Yes ☐ No ☐	Yes ☐ No ☐	Yes ☐ No ☐	Yes ☐ No ☐

Je ne sais quoi

What exactly makes your lover so lovable? Is it an aura? Is it a "special something"? Is it a million imperceptible things? Do try to narrow it down a little, or you can't say you really know them. Pinpoint the secret of their appeal.

Affix photo of him taken while sleeping, and circle the features you consider particularly alluring

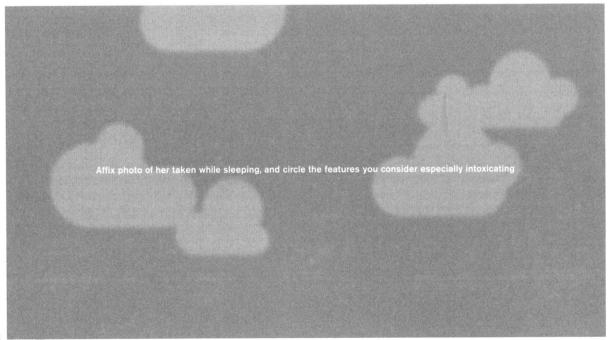

Affix photo of her taken while sleeping, and circle the features you consider especially intoxicating

Secret of their appeal (5 maximum)

Is it the way they bat their eyelids first thing in the morning?	☐	Is it the way they still get scared by lightning?	☐
Is it the way they smile when they see a kitten?	☐	Is it the way they can't drive and talk at the same time?	☐
Is it the way they tell you off for not straightening the bed clothes?	☐	Is it the way they run up the stairs?	☐
Is it the way they wiggle their little toes when they're excited?	☐	Is it the way they speak to their grandmother?	☐
Is it the way they sigh at the world news?	☐	Is it the way they splash around in the bath?	☐
Is it the way they frown when they're angry?	☐	Is it the way they snuggle up to you under the duvet?	☐
Is it the way they never confess to being lost?	☐	Is it the way they munch through pizza?	☐
Is it the way they ruffle their hair?	☐	Is it the way they always kiss you at the movies?	☐
Is it the way they squeeze the toothpaste to death?	☐	Is it the way they flirt with your parents?	☐
Is it the way they sometimes laugh in their sleep?	☐	Is it the way they strut around the garden?	☐
Is it the way they look in pyjamas?	☐	Is it the way they grin at babies?	☐
Is it the way they jump over puddles?	☐	Is it the way they keep a collection of photos of you?	☐
Is it the way they pick their nose when they think you're not looking?	☐	Is it the way they blow on their hot soup?	☐
Is it the way they cuddle you when they're drunk?	☐	Is it the way they tie their shoelaces?	☐
Is it the way they undress while looking you in the eye?	☐	Is it the way they whisper "I love you"?	☐
Is it the way they sing your name in the shower?	☐	Is it the way they sniff at the breeze?	☐
Is it the way they never remember to tuck their shirt label in?	☐	Is it the way they still open doors for you?	☐
Is it the way they always seem surprised by snow?	☐	Is it the way they try to surprise you?	☐
Is it the way they concentrate to comb their hair?	☐	Is it the way they can't cook to save their life?	☐
Is it the way they never read the menu until the waiter arrives?	☐	Is it the way they get freckles in the spring?	☐
Is it the way they squint at sunsets?	☐	Is it the way they care about the colour of their bubblegum?	☐
Is it the way they still play with their food?	☐	Is it the way they talk to children?	☐
Is it the way they refuse to hurt a fly?	☐	Is it the way they brush their teeth one by one?	☐
Is it the way they laugh at unfunny jokes?	☐	Is it the way they close their eyes when they're counting?	☐
Is it the way they seek your hand in a crowd?	☐	Is it the way they look at people who don't like you?	☐
Is it the way they pretend to agree with you when you're wrong?	☐	Is it the way they run to try and escape the rain?	☐
Is it the way they never remember anyone's name save yours?	☐	Is it the way they like probing your belly button?	☐
Is it the way they talk to the television screen?	☐	Is it the way they keep losing umbrellas?	☐
Is it the way they collect autumn leaves?	☐	Is it the way they go red when they're guilty?	☐
Is it the way they stroke stray cats?	☐	Is it the way they still mourn their first teddy bear?	☐

Metaphors for your lover

Are they like a ray of sunshine on a winter morning?	Yes ☐ No ☐ Occasionally ☐
Are they like a breath of fresh air?	Yes ☐ No ☐ Occasionally ☐
Are they like a twinkle in the eye of a child?	Yes ☐ No ☐ Occasionally ☐
Are they like a shooting star on the horizon?	Yes ☐ No ☐ Occasionally ☐
Are they like a volcano erupting in your heart?	Yes ☐ No ☐ Occasionally ☐
Are they like a sparrow chirping at the new dawn?	Yes ☐ No ☐ Occasionally ☐
Are they like a snowflake melting in your hand?	Yes ☐ No ☐ Occasionally ☐
Are they like a rainbow clearing the air?	Yes ☐ No ☐ Occasionally ☐
Are they like a rush of adrenalin to the head?	Yes ☐ No ☐ Occasionally ☐
Are they like a storm gathering over the horizon?	Yes ☐ No ☐ Occasionally ☐
Are they like a sleeping tiger waiting to be roused?	Yes ☐ No ☐ Occasionally ☐
Are they like a scorpion stinging you out of fear?	Yes ☐ No ☐ Occasionally ☐
Are they like an octopus strangling you with their love?	Yes ☐ No ☐ Occasionally ☐
Are they like a tidal wave overpowering your defences?	Yes ☐ No ☐ Occasionally ☐
Are they like a tornado laying waste to your soul?	Yes ☐ No ☐ Occasionally ☐
Are they like a black hole sucking in your emotions?	Yes ☐ No ☐ Occasionally ☐

Things that your lover is *not* like

Knife	☐	Stapler	☐	Button	☐	Camera	☐	Boot	☐
Superglue	☐	Chair	☐	Bush	☐	Vase	☐	Sofa	☐
Boiled egg	☐	Pen	☐	Gate	☐	Cheese	☐	TV	☐
Biscuit	☐	Cup of tea	☐	Crayon	☐	Slipper	☐	Envelope	☐
Weed	☐	Sponge	☐	Suitcase	☐	Doughnut	☐	Bench	☐
Catapult	☐	Plane	☐	Ball	☐	Soap	☐	Padlock	☐
Lightbulb	☐	Plug	☐	Plastic bag	☐	Potato	☐	Elevator	☐

Words of wisdom 4

Søren ponders: "I have known Karen 71 years. It is impossible for me to say, why I like her. I know it is not her dancing, that much is for safe. She is like a peasant, a big clod, a sea-turtle. I am a butterfly near her. At the Jalberg dance, the boys would make run far, even if she was so beautiful. Anybody at all could never explain how some such beautiful creature was such an elephant! But if you leave these things, you disturb you, you will divorce for sure. Expensive."

Deepest secrets

Absolute intimacy is an illusion. There are things that
you may never know about your love, secrets which
you must trust each other to respect. Write them here
and follow the instructions to seal your page forever.

Her deepest secrets

Secret 1:..
....
....
....

How deep is this secret?   How long have you kept this secret?...

Top secret □   Very secret □   Does anyone else know about this secret?...

Pretty secret □   Secret-ish □   What will you do if this secret comes out?...

Secret 2:..
....
....
....

How deep is this secret?   How long have you kept this secret?...

Top secret □   Very secret □   Does anyone else know about this secret?...

Pretty secret □   Secret-ish □   What will you do if this secret comes out?...

Secret 3:..
....
....
....

How deep is this secret?   How long have you kept this secret?...

Top secret □   Very secret □   Does anyone else know about this secret?...

Pretty secret □   Secret-ish □   What will you do if this secret comes out?...

What I'm afraid   I'm shallow □ I'm superficial □ I'm stupid □ I'm boring □ I'm too thin □ I'm too fat □
you'll notice   I'm ugly □ I'm a bad person □ I'm not good enough for you □ I'm insecure □
someday   Who is to blame for these insecurities? Parents □ Other □ (specify:............................)

Once you have written your secrets, fold the page and superglue it all along its length. If you do not fully trust your partner, you may want to place a strain of hair as shown, so you can check if your secrets have been tampered with. Keep an eye out for other clues such as your partner storming out inexplicably.

His deepest secrets

Secret 1:..
....
....
....

How deep is this secret?   How long have you kept this secret?..

Top secret ☐   Very secret ☐   Does anyone else know about this secret?...

Pretty secret ☐ Secret-ish ☐   What will you do if this secret comes out?..

Secret 2:..
....
....
....

How deep is this secret?   How long have you kept this secret?..

Top secret ☐   Very secret ☐   Does anyone else know about this secret?...

Pretty secret ☐ Secret-ish ☐   What will you do if this secret comes out?..

Secret 3:..
....
....
....

How deep is this secret?   How long have you kept this secret?..

Top secret ☐   Very secret ☐   Does anyone else know about this secret?...

Pretty secret ☐ Secret-ish ☐   What will you do if this secret comes out?..

What I'm afraid   I'm shallow ☐ I'm superficial ☐ I'm stupid ☐ I'm boring ☐ I'm too thin ☐ I'm too fat ☐
you'll notice   I'm ugly ☐ I'm a bad person ☐ I'm not good enough for you ☐ I'm insecure ☐
someday   Who is to blame for these insecurities? Parents ☐ Other ☐ (specify:............................)

Commitment

Only read this chapter when you are both ready. It addresses such matters as marriage, children, and who does the washing up. This is perhaps the unglamorous side of love, but if your relationship is to be more than just a flash in the pan, you will need to deal with it.

Marriage material

Eternal romance is for teenagers. By entering this chapter, you are leaving the happy-go-lucky phase of your relationship, and are now heading firmly for the 2.4 kids stretch. Monitor how ready you are to tie the knot.

Take it in turns to add a good reason to marry, as per our example. When your reasons have added up to reach the little church, you are ready!

She's a breath of fresh air

He's so good with kids

Her risottos are divine

He's such a great dancer

I'm never going to do better than her

He's definitely an alpha male etc.

Benrik practice engagement ring: Cut out a practice ring in your size and wear it for a few days. Could you get used to it?

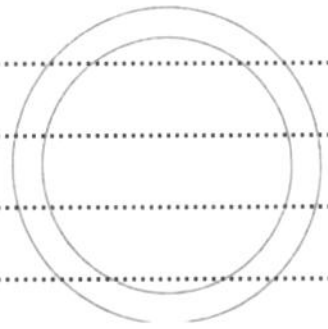

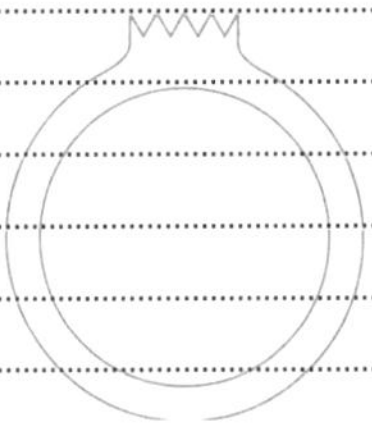

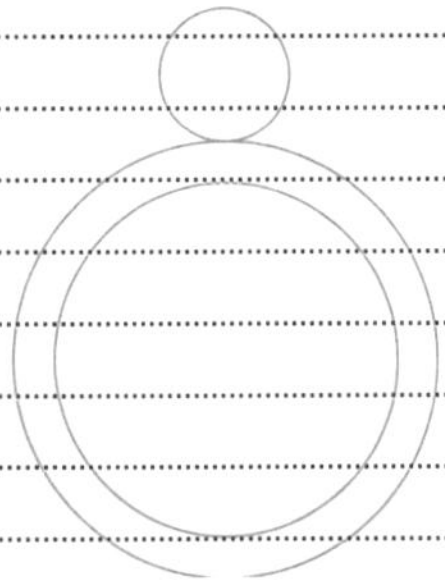

Woman
Use his surname instead of yours, however inconvenient, and insist on being called Mrs.

Man
Refer to "my wife", "my ladywife" or "my better half" in every conversation.

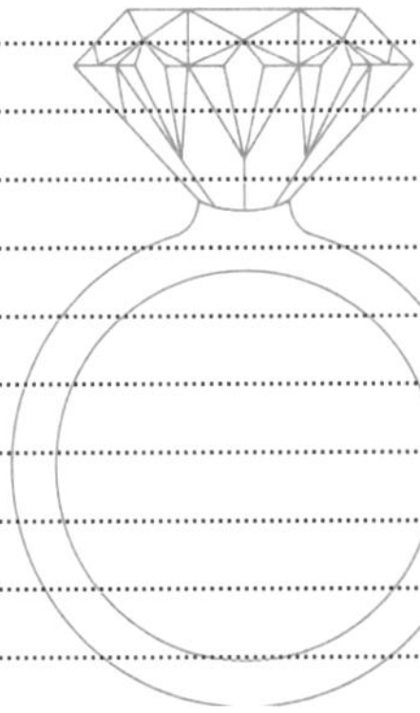

Baby practice module
Stare at this picture for 24 hours in a row. Do not leave the room. Do not fall asleep. Be attentive to its every detail. And above all, keep it entertained.

The Little Church

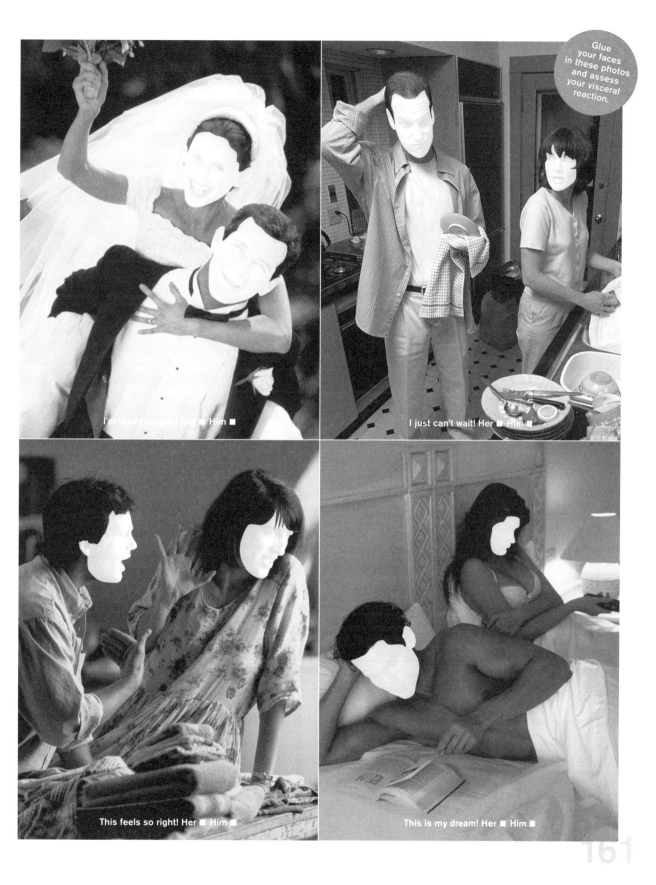

Glue your faces in these photos and assess your visceral reaction.

I'm ready for this! Her ■ Him ■

I just can't wait! Her ■ Him ■

This feels so right! Her ■ Him ■

This is my dream! Her ■ Him ■

161

Compatibility

A study recently revealed that the best predictor of divorce was opposing views on two key subjects: politics and pornography. Before proceeding any further in life together, check you are not fatally split on the following major issues.

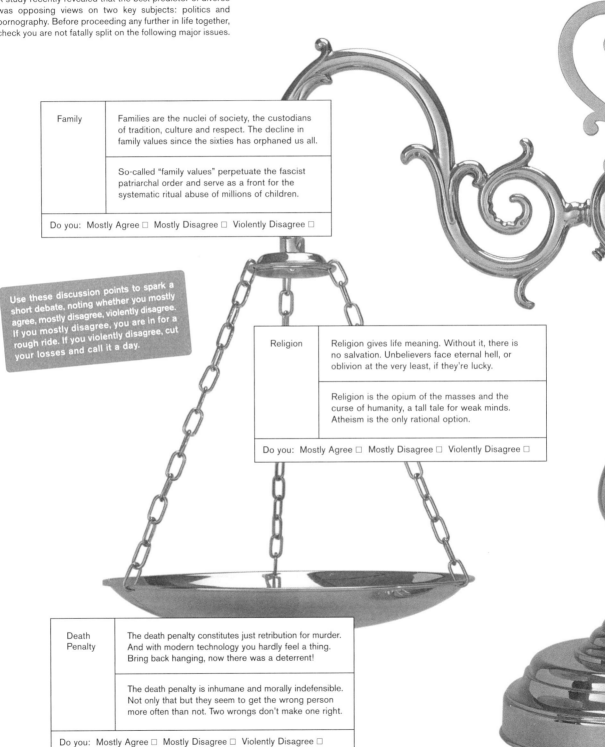

Family	Families are the nuclei of society, the custodians of tradition, culture and respect. The decline in family values since the sixties has orphaned us all.
	So-called "family values" perpetuate the fascist patriarchal order and serve as a front for the systematic ritual abuse of millions of children.
Do you: Mostly Agree ☐ Mostly Disagree ☐ Violently Disagree ☐	

Use these discussion points to spark a short debate, noting whether you mostly agree, mostly disagree, violently disagree. If you mostly disagree, you are in for a rough ride. If you violently disagree, cut your losses and call it a day.

Religion	Religion gives life meaning. Without it, there is no salvation. Unbelievers face eternal hell, or oblivion at the very least, if they're lucky.
	Religion is the opium of the masses and the curse of humanity, a tall tale for weak minds. Atheism is the only rational option.
Do you: Mostly Agree ☐ Mostly Disagree ☐ Violently Disagree ☐	

Death Penalty	The death penalty constitutes just retribution for murder. And with modern technology you hardly feel a thing. Bring back hanging, now there was a deterrent!
	The death penalty is inhumane and morally indefensible. Not only that but they seem to get the wrong person more often than not. Two wrongs don't make one right.
Do you: Mostly Agree ☐ Mostly Disagree ☐ Violently Disagree ☐	

| Politics | Capitalism is the only effective form of social organization, and will in due course liberate most of the world from poverty and repression. |
| | Globalization is a sham. The poor get poorer while the rich get richer. Oil companies are cynical profiteers. And fat cats rule the world. |

Do you: Mostly Agree ☐ Mostly Disagree ☐ Violently Disagree ☐

Words of wisdom 5

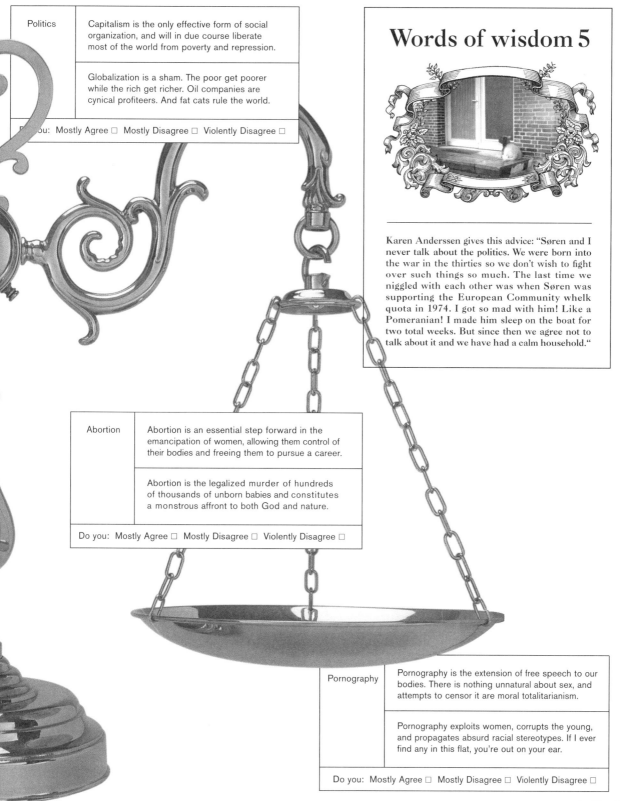

Karen Anderssen gives this advice: "Søren and I never talk about the politics. We were born into the war in the thirties so we don't wish to fight over such things so much. The last time we niggled with each other was when Søren was supporting the European Community whelk quota in 1974. I got so mad with him! Like a Pomeranian! I made him sleep on the boat for two total weeks. But since then we agree not to talk about it and we have had a calm household."

| Abortion | Abortion is an essential step forward in the emancipation of women, allowing them control of their bodies and freeing them to pursue a career. |
| | Abortion is the legalized murder of hundreds of thousands of unborn babies and constitutes a monstrous affront to both God and nature. |

Do you: Mostly Agree ☐ Mostly Disagree ☐ Violently Disagree ☐

| Pornography | Pornography is the extension of free speech to our bodies. There is nothing unnatural about sex, and attempts to censor it are moral totalitarianism. |
| | Pornography exploits women, corrupts the young, and propagates absurd racial stereotypes. If I ever find any in this flat, you're out on your ear. |

Do you: Mostly Agree ☐ Mostly Disagree ☐ Violently Disagree ☐

163

The Couple's Moodchart

The trained couple will not wait for issues to emerge, but will scrutinize each other's mood for oncoming squalls, much as the sailor does the horizon. Use this mood chart daily to monitor the ebb and flow of your relationship.

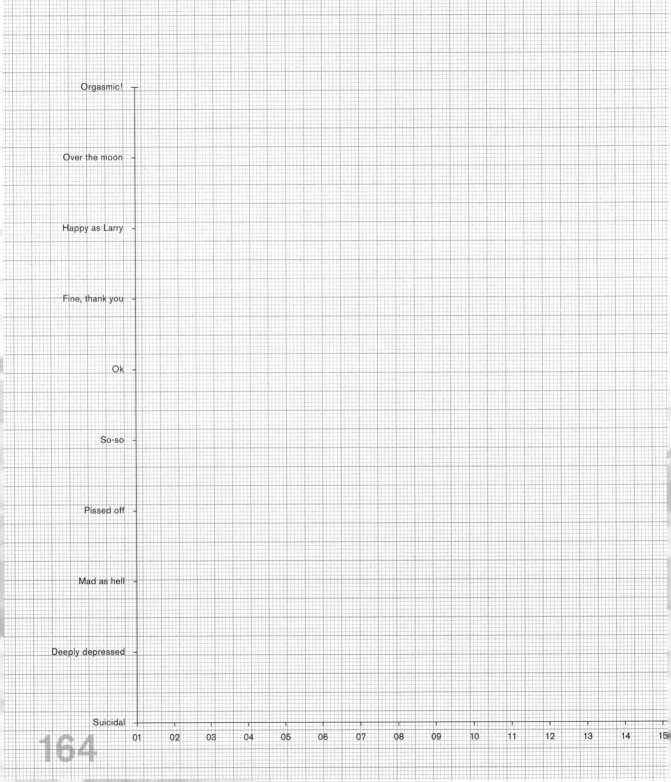

Orgasmic!

Over the moon

Happy as Larry

Fine, thank you

Ok

So-so

Pissed off

Mad as hell

Deeply depressed

Suicidal

01 02 03 04 05 06 07 08 09 10 11 12 13 14 15

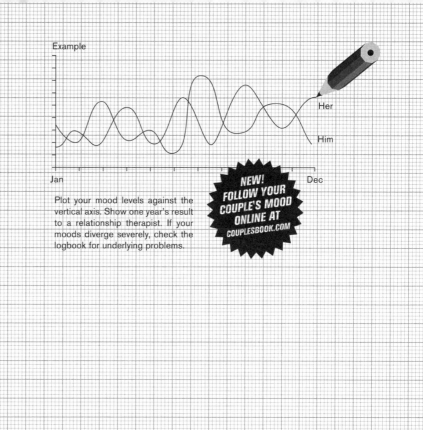

Example

Her

Him

Jan   Dec

Plot your mood levels against the vertical axis. Show one year's result to a relationship therapist. If your moods diverge severely, check the logbook for underlying problems.

Household chores

A considerable proportion of your logbook complaints will be about this sorest of points. Here is a handy weekly rota system to help you manage chores fairly and harmoniously. Write your names in the relevant spaces and sign below.

	Monday	Tuesday	Wednesday
Washing up			
Laundry			
Vacuuming			
Making the bed			
Changing the sheets			
Cleaning the toilet			
Dusting			
Sweeping			
Emptying the bins			
Taking the rubbish out			
Mowing the lawn			
Walking the dog			
Feeding the dog			
Plumping the cushions			
Cleaning the windows			
Putting up the shelves			
Polishing the silverware			
Changing dead lightbulbs			
Buying toilet rolls			
Washing the car			
Scrubbing the grout			
Picking up the dead flies			
Ironing			
Recycling			
Watering the geraniums			
Sorting out the sock drawer			
Other			

Her Signature: ....

Thursday   Friday   Saturday   Sunday

His Signature:..

Material possessions

In our consumerist society, buying vast quantities of material goods
together is as much an expression of commitment as having children.
It is also the source of much heartbreak when you split up. Keep this
to a minimum by recording who bought what, when, and where.

Books	Cost	Date	Who suggested this purchase			Share of cost		Shopkeeper's signature	Bad taste. I strongly disagreed with this purchase and refuse to have it displayed in our common living area.		Comment
			Her	Him	Both	Her	Him		She	He	

CDs

Cars

| DVDs | Cost | Date | Who suggested this purchase | | | Share of cost | | Shopkeeper's signature | | Bad taste. I strongly disagreed with this purchase and refuse to have it displayed in our common living area. | | |
			Her	Him	Both	Her	Him			She	He	Comment
Furniture												
Junk												

Money matters

Love may be free, but life is expensive. Couples can at least share some of the costs, although not without much recrimination in the process. Try and avoid it by using our Couple's Book financial spreadsheet. Take a couple of hours to plan your financial future now, so you don't have to worry about it ever again.

Year	01	02	03	04	05	06	07	08	09	10	11	12	13	14	15	16	17	18	19	20	21	22	23	24	25	26	27	2
Income																												
Her salary																												
Investment																												
Inheritance																												
Other																												
Expenditure																												
Fixed expenses																												
Mortgage/rent																												
Car payments																												
Electricity																												
Water																												
Local taxes																												
Cable TV/internet																												
Buildings insurance																												
Medical insurance																												
Auto insurance																												
Personal loan																												
Pension plan																												
Variable expenses																												
Drink																												
Clothing																												
Other travel expenses																												
School																												
Memberships																												
Books																												
Eating out																												
Pet care																												
Gifts to each other																												
Her pocket money																												
Total variable expenses																												
Income minus expenses																												

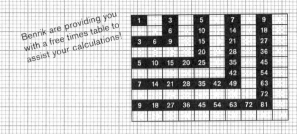

Benrik are providing you with a free times table to assist your calculations!

1		3		5		7		9
			6		10		14		18
3	6	9			15		21		27
			20			28		36
5	10	15	20	25		35		45
						42		54
7	14	21	28	35	42	49		63
								72
9	18	27	36	45	54	63	72	81

| 29 | 30 | 31 | 32 | 33 | 34 | 35 | 36 | 37 | 38 | 39 | 40 | 41 | 42 | 43 | 44 | 45 | 46 | 47 | 48 | 49 | 50 | 51 | 52 | 53 | 54 | 55 | 56 | 57 | 58 | 59 | 60 |

171

Hygiene

In the early days you may have tolerated odd habits and nasty smells, but now that you are settling down, you have a chance to change them. Root out each other's more unsavoury routines and improve your joint appearance.

Problem:..

Proposed solution:....................................

Progress report:.......................................

Problem solved? Yes ☐ No ☐

Problem:..

Proposed solution:....................................

Progress report:.......................................

Problem solved? Yes ☐ No ☐

Her wardrobe reviewed

Clothes of yours I don't like:..
....
....
I demand that you discard your revolting...................
....
....
immediately, or I refuse to go out with you in public.

Problem:..
Proposed solution:..............................
Progress report:.................................
Problem solved? Yes ☐ No ☐

Problem:..
Proposed solution:..............................
Progress report:.................................
Problem solved? Yes ☐ No ☐

Problem:..
Proposed solution:..............................
Progress report:.................................
Problem solved? Yes ☐ No ☐

Problem:..
Proposed solution:..............................
Progress report:.................................
Problem solved? Yes ☐ No ☐

Problem:..
Proposed solution:..............................
Progress report:.................................
Problem solved? Yes ☐ No ☐

Problem:..
Proposed solution:..............................
Progress report:.................................
Problem solved? Yes ☐ No ☐

Problem:..
Proposed solution:..............................
Progress report:.................................
Problem solved? Yes ☐ No ☐

Problem:..
Proposed solution:..............................
Progress report:.................................
Problem solved? Yes ☐ No ☐

Problem:..
Proposed solution:..............................
Progress report:.................................
Problem solved? Yes ☐ No ☐

Problem:..
Proposed solution:..............................
Progress report:.................................
Problem solved? Yes ☐ No ☐

Problem:..
Proposed solution:..............................
Progress report:.................................
Problem solved? Yes ☐ No ☐

His wardrobe reviewed

Clothes of yours I don't like:...
....
....
I demand that you discard your revolting.....................
....
....
immediately, or I refuse to go out with you in public.

173

Comfort zones

Couples trust each other to respect certain rules of behaviour. Most of these are unspoken, though, which can lead to misunderstandings. Spell out the limits of your comfort zones, so you don't scupper the relationship unintentionally.

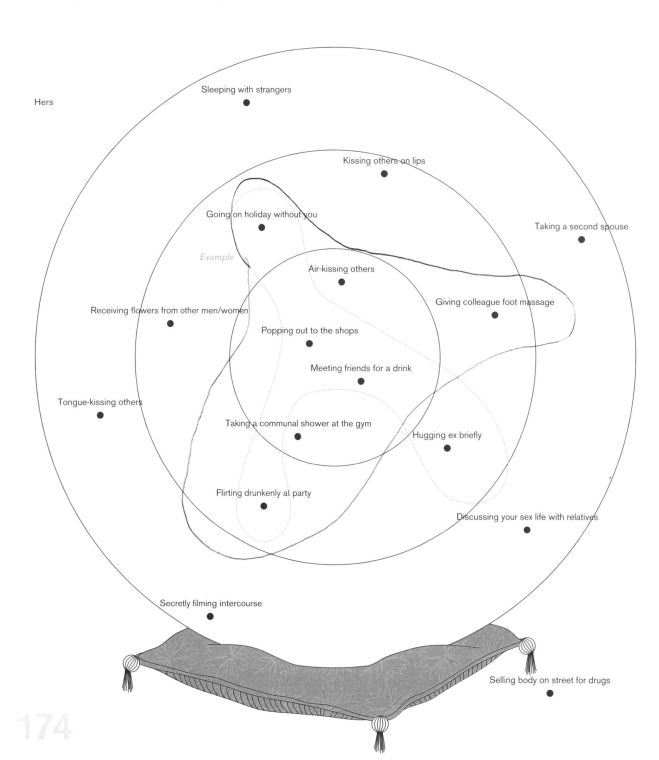

Hers

Sleeping with strangers

Kissing others on lips

Going on holiday without you

Taking a second spouse

Example

Air-kissing others

Giving colleague foot massage

Receiving flowers from other men/women

Popping out to the shops

Meeting friends for a drink

Tongue-kissing others

Taking a communal shower at the gym

Hugging ex briefly

Flirting drunkenly at party

Discussing your sex life with relatives

Secretly filming intercourse

Selling body on street for drugs

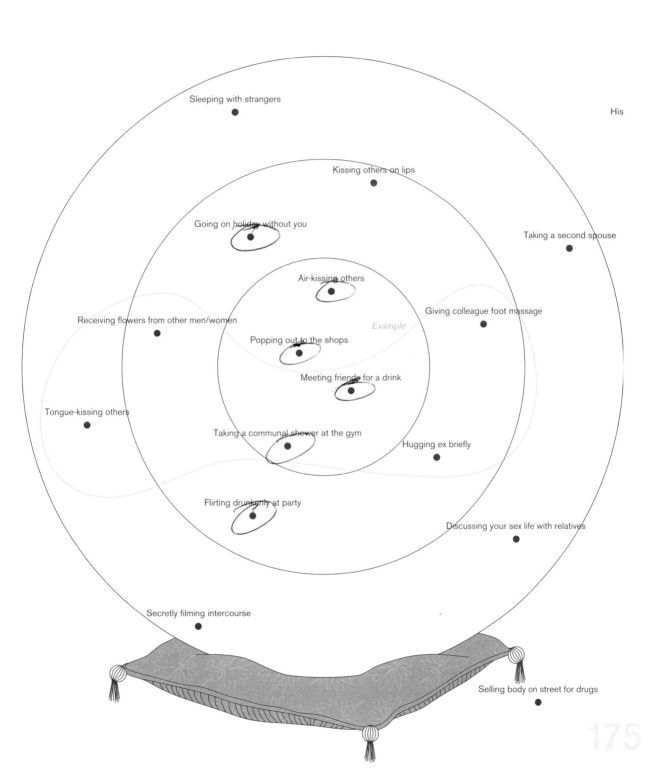

Sleeping with strangers

His

Kissing others on lips

Going on holiday without you

Taking a second spouse

Air-kissing others

Receiving flowers from other men/women

Giving colleague foot massage

Example

Popping out to the shops

Meeting friends for a drink

Tongue-kissing others

Taking a communal shower at the gym

Hugging ex briefly

Flirting drunkenly at party

Discussing your sex life with relatives

Secretly filming intercourse

Selling body on street for drugs

Open relationships

Lifelong sexual fidelity may not suit everyone. For the more Scandinavian-minded amongst you, here is a handy aid to help manage your open relationship. To make a success of it, you will need clearly-established rules. Freedom yes, free-for-all no.

Her other relationships

Name..	Name..	Name..
Age..	Age..	Age..
Start date.................................	Start date.................................	Start date.................................
How often we have sex...............	How often we have sex...............	How often we have sex...............
This relationship is vetoed! ☐	This relationship is vetoed! ☐	This relationship is vetoed! ☐
Name..	Name..	Name..
Age..	Age..	Age..
Start date.................................	Start date.................................	Start date.................................
How often we have sex...............	How often we have sex...............	How often we have sex...............
This relationship is vetoed! ☐	This relationship is vetoed! ☐	This relationship is vetoed! ☐
Name..	Name..	Name..
Age..	Age..	Age..
Start date.................................	Start date.................................	Start date.................................
How often we have sex...............	How often we have sex...............	How often we have sex...............
This relationship is vetoed! ☐	This relationship is vetoed! ☐	This relationship is vetoed! ☐
Name..	Name..	Name..
Age..	Age..	Age..
Start date.................................	Start date.................................	Start date.................................
How often we have sex...............	How often we have sex...............	How often we have sex...............
This relationship is vetoed! ☐	This relationship is vetoed! ☐	This relationship is vetoed! ☐
Name..	Name..	Name..
Age..	Age..	Age..
Start date.................................	Start date.................................	Start date.................................
How often we have sex...............	How often we have sex...............	How often we have sex...............
This relationship is vetoed! ☐	This relationship is vetoed! ☐	This relationship is vetoed! ☐

Rules: Our open relationship will operate in accordance with the following rules.
We each have the power of veto Yes ■ No ■
We must tell each other Yes ■ No ■
We don't want to know Yes ■ No ■
We are allowed to spend nights with them Yes ■ No ■
We are allowed to bring them home Yes ■ No ■
We are allowed to fall in love with them Yes ■ No ■
Maximum number.. per month/year
Maximum hours spent per week..

"NO-NO" LIST

We are not allowed relationships with:
Escorts ■
Intravenous drug users ■
Each other's best friend ■
Each other's relatives ■
Other:..■

His other relationships

Name............................	Name............................	Name............................
Age............................	Age............................	Age............................
Start date............................	Start date............................	Start date............................
How often we have sex............	How often we have sex............	How often we have sex............
This relationship is vetoed! ☐	This relationship is vetoed! ☐	This relationship is vetoed! ☐
Name............................	Name............................	Name............................
Age............................	Age............................	Age............................
Start date............................	Start date............................	Start date............................
How often we have sex............	How often we have sex............	How often we have sex............
This relationship is vetoed! ☐	This relationship is vetoed! ☐	This relationship is vetoed! ☐
Name............................	Name............................	Name............................
Age............................	Age............................	Age............................
Start date............................	Start date............................	Start date............................
How often we have sex............	How often we have sex............	How often we have sex............
This relationship is vetoed! ☐	This relationship is vetoed! ☐	This relationship is vetoed! ☐
Name............................	Name............................	Name............................
Age............................	Age............................	Age............................
Start date............................	Start date............................	Start date............................
How often we have sex............	How often we have sex............	How often we have sex............
This relationship is vetoed! ☐	This relationship is vetoed! ☐	This relationship is vetoed! ☐
Name............................	Name............................	Name............................
Age............................	Age............................	Age............................
Start date............................	Start date............................	Start date............................
How often we have sex............	How often we have sex............	How often we have sex............
This relationship is vetoed! ☐	This relationship is vetoed! ☐	This relationship is vetoed! ☐

Proposal

To attain complete coupled-up bliss, you must eventually get married. Go about this the wrong way, however, and divorce may shortly follow. Make sure you employ the standard proposal procedure outlined here to maximize your chances of success.

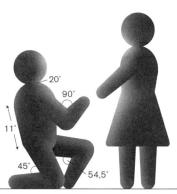

---

1. Proposal: ● ○ ○ ○

Dear girlfriend/boyfriend

....(insert name),

Will you marry me?

Supporting arguments (e.g. "I love you lots"):

1)...

and 2)...

and 3)...

and 4)...("clincher" argument)

---

2. Spontaneous reaction: ● ● ○ ○

Yes □

Comments: Whohoo! □ Why not □ I thought you'd never ask □

Other □ (specify):...

....

No □

Reason: I'm not ready □ I don't love you □ I love someone else □

I don't know you □ Other □ (specify):..................................

....

---

3. Hesitation: ● ● ● ○

Ask the proposer for a few minutes to think, and discreetly try out these decision-making aids:

Eenie Meenie Minie Mo

Result: Yes □ No □ Ambiguous □

---

4. Final decision: ● ● ● ●

Accepted!   □

Rejected...   □

Postponed   □ (try again in six months' time)

Prenuptial Agreement:

Benrik's lawyers have drafted a legally binding prenuptial agreement that you may use free of charge.

To whom it may concern, this agreement is entered into on this................ day of................ 20.............,
between.. and..

Whereas the prospective spouses intend to marry under the laws of ....,
and wish to enter into this agreement so that they will continue to own and control their own property,
and are getting married because of their love for each other, but do not desire that their present
respective financial interests be changed by their marriage.

Whereas, the parties have made to each other a full disclosure of their assets, as set forth below.

Whereas, both parties have been independently represented and have received a full and complete
explanation of their rights, the consequences of entering into this legal arrangement, and the rights
they relinquish thereby.

It is, therefore, now agreed as follows.

1) All property belonging to each of the above parties shall be, and shall forever remain, their personal
estate, including all monies accruing from said property.

2) Both parties agree that they each retain the right to sell, dispose of, use, enjoy, encumber, gift and
convey their separate property as freely as if the marriage had never taken place.

3) Both parties agree that in the event of separation or divorce, the parties shall have no right against
each other's property, but each shall retain his or her property. Joint property is to be equally divided.
Both parties agree to waive their claims for support, maintenance, alimony, inheritance, compensation
in the estates of each other.

4) Both parties are advised that prenuptial agreements waiving these rights are only legally binding if
entered into free from any form of pressure, coercion or duress, and with full and complete disclosure
of assets at the date of marriage.

5) This agreement shall be binding on the parties, their children, successors, legatees, assigns and
representatives of both parties.

6) This agreement shall be enforced under the law of England and Wales at the time of this agreement.

Signature of Fiancé... Date...................................
Signature of Fiancée... Date...................................
Witness... Date...................................
Witness... Date...................................

Wedding location planner

No one simply gets married down their childhood church one rainy afternoon any more. You must impress the strength of your love on your friends and family by scheduling a months-long list of events across the globe. Otherwise no one will come.

Event	Location	Month

Last Year's Wedding Musts!

Event	Location	Month
Engagement party	Paris	October
Stag do	Barcelona	February
Hen do	Edinburgh	March
Civil ceremony	Bath	May
Church ceremony	Gothenburg	July
Honeymoon	Bahamas	August

Make it special, and those long-lost relatives will travel!

The big day

After the day you were born and the day that you'll die, this is the most important day of your life. It's also the only one of the three you'll actually enjoy, so plan well ahead and make your Couple's Book an integral part of the ceremony.

Date..

Time..

Phase of the moon:

Location

Budget: Who is paying what?

Bride's parents..

Groom's parents..

Bride & Groom...

Rich uncle..

Corporate sponsors (specify).....................................

Total planned cost............... Total final cost...............

Guest list	Bride	Groom
A-list (ceremony reception & dinner)		
B-list (ceremony & reception)		
C-list (reception only)		
Distant relatives (false address on invitation)		

The Dress

Colour:
White ☐
Cream ☐
Blue ☐
Pink ☐
Mauve ☐
Black ☐

Checklist:
Something old ☐
Something new ☐
Something borrowed ☐
Something blue ☐

Warning! No peeking from the groom!

Parents

Parents may use this space to help plan the happy occasion. In addition they may interfere by scribbling over any other part of these pages.

....

....

....

....

Grumblings about unsuitability of the match:

....

The Couple's Book is the responsibility of the Chief Bridesmaid on the day of the wedding. She should carry it to the altar and hand it over to the Minister, who alone is authorized to complete the details below.

Chief Bridesmaid...

Secondary Bridesmaids..

Best Man...

Hand the Couple's Book over to Minister

Minister...

Name...

Church...

Qualifications..

Minister: We are gathered here today to witness the joining together in holy matrimony of ....(bride's first name) and ....(groom's first name). First, does anyone here know of any reason why this marriage should not take place?

Objections

1.. Objection accepted? Yes ☐ No ☐

2.. Objection accepted? Yes ☐ No ☐

3.. Objection accepted? Yes ☐ No ☐

Minister to bride: Do you,..(bride's name), take ....(groom's name) to be your lawful wedded husband? Do you promise to love him, comfort him, honour and protect him, and, forsaking all others, be faithful to him as long as you both shall live?

Record bride's response: I do ☐ I don't ☐ Other (specify):......................
....

Minister to groom: Do you,..(groom's name), take ....(bride's name) to be your lawful wedded wife? Do you promise to love her, comfort her, honour and protect her, and, forsaking all others, be faithful to her as long as you both shall live?

Record groom's response: I do ☐ I don't ☐ Other (specify):...................
....

	Bride	Groom
For better	Yes ☐ No ☐	Yes ☐ No ☐
For worse	Yes ☐ No ☐	Yes ☐ No ☐
For richer	Yes ☐ No ☐	Yes ☐ No ☐
For poorer	Yes ☐ No ☐	Yes ☐ No ☐
In sickness	Yes ☐ No ☐	Yes ☐ No ☐
In health	Yes ☐ No ☐	Yes ☐ No ☐
To love	Yes ☐ No ☐	Yes ☐ No ☐
To cherish	Yes ☐ No ☐	Yes ☐ No ☐
Till death us do part	Yes ☐ No ☐	Yes ☐ No ☐

This section is based on C of E standard ritual. You are free to adapt it to your religious persuasion or sexual orientation.

The Wedding Cake

How many layers? 1 ☐ 2 ☐ 3 ☐ 4 ☐ 5 ☐ 6 ☐

Who got the bouquet?

....

....

Married one year later? Yes ☐ No ☐

Shotgun weddings only

Motive: Pregnant ☐ Drunk ☐ Elopement ☐ Underage ☐
Already married ☐ Other ☐ (specify).....................
....

Location: Vegas ☐ Other ☐ (specify)................................
....

Honeymoon

Destination:..

Duration:..

Level of blissfulness:../10

The Couple's Book must accompany you on honeymoon or your marriage will be cursed. Benrik also reserve the right to come along.

Groom signature:..

Bride signature:..

Minister signature:..

Minister to congregation: I pronounce this couple husband and wife!

Cue music:...

Making babies

If you want to start a family, you will need to produce babies. To make them, refer to the "Pillow Talk" chapter, ignoring any contraceptive advice. These pages deal with the less immediately enjoyable aspects of raising children.

Biological clock

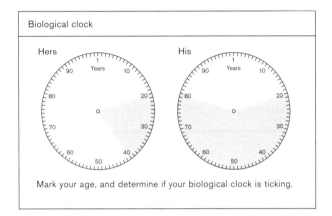

Hers
His

Mark your age, and determine if your biological clock is ticking.

Benrik Pregnancy Test: Deposit a drop of urine on this specially treated surface. If it turns blue within one minute, you're pregnant!

Her Yes ☐ No ☐   Him Yes ☐ No ☐

Every child should be entitled to know the glorious circumstances of their conception: record the exact time & date of intercourse and present them with the details as a lovely surprise on their 16th birthday.

Conception Certificate
no1!

Dear.. (child's name),

You were conceived at...........................(time) on the

.......................(date) at...(place).

Your parents were in bed ☐ on the sofa ☐

on the kitchen floor ☐ other (specify)...................☐,

in the.. position.

The sex was great ☐ good ☐ ok ☐ drunken ☐.

Your conception was deliberate ☐ an accident ☐.

There is a photographic ☐ videographic ☐ record

of it which you may view when you are 21.

Happy 16th Birthday! Mummy & Daddy

Child 1
Girl ☐
Boy ☐

Photo

Name..
Rejected name...................................
Date of Birth........../........../.........
Time of Birth.......................................
Pain of Birth............................./10
First word:...

Child 2
Girl ☐
Boy ☐

Photo

Name..
Rejected name...................................
Date of Birth........../........../.........
Time of Birth.......................................
Pain of Birth............................./10
First word:...

Child 3
Girl ☐
Boy ☐

Photo

Name..
Rejected name...................................
Date of Birth........../........../.........
Time of Birth.......................................
Pain of Birth............................./10
First word:...

Child 4
Girl ☐
Boy ☐

Photo

Name..
Rejected name...................................
Date of Birth........../........../.........
Time of Birth.......................................
Pain of Birth............................./10
First word:...

Which child is your favourite?

Her favourite.. His favourite..

Baby chores:	Monday	Tuesday	Wednesday	Thursday	Friday	Saturday	Sunday
Changing nappies							
Cleaning up vomit							
Dressing the baby							
Bathing the baby							
Burping the baby							
Amusing the baby							
Cooing							
Breastfeeding at 3a.m.	*Her*	*Her*	*Her*	*Her*	*Her*	*Her*	*Her*

Sex counter	
January	Yes ☐ No ☐
February	Yes ☐ No ☐
March	Yes ☐ No ☐
April	Yes ☐ No ☐
May	Yes ☐ No ☐
June	Yes ☐ No ☐
July	Yes ☐ No ☐
August	Yes ☐ No ☐
September	Yes ☐ No ☐
October	Yes ☐ No ☐
November	Yes ☐ No ☐
December	Yes ☐ No ☐

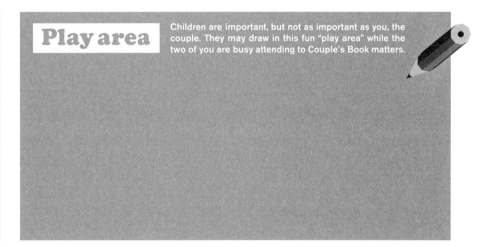

Play area

Children are important, but not as important as you, the couple. They may draw in this fun "play area" while the two of you are busy attending to Couple's Book matters.

Telling your child about the birds and the bees

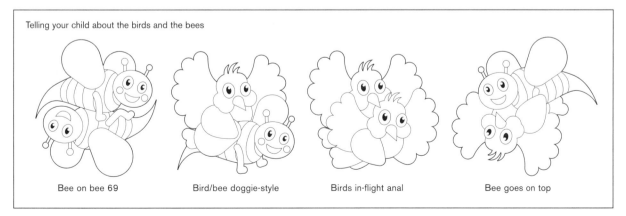

Bee on bee 69   Bird/bee doggie-style   Birds in-flight anal   Bee goes on top

Who inherits the Couple's Book The Couple's Book is a prized heirloom that children often fight over after the couple's death. To avert this painful and undignified scenario, Benrik have introduced a simple rule: the child that cost the least to raise inherits the book.

How are we doing?

Couples can drift apart out of sheer inertia, with both parties waking up one day to the realization that it's over. Subject your relationship to an annual check-up throughout its life, and reverse any downward trends as soon as they emerge.

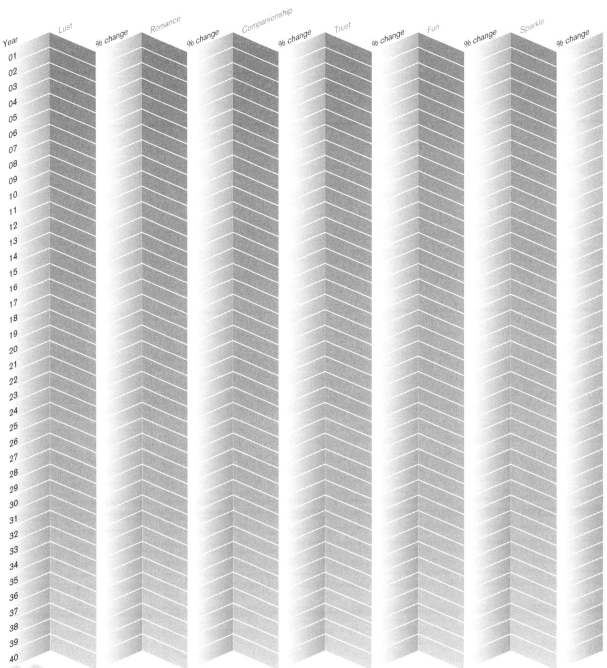

Year · Lust · % change · Romance · % change · Companionship · % change · Trust · % change · Fun · % change · Sparkle · % change

01 02 03 04 05 06 07 08 09 10 11 12 13 14 15 16 17 18 19 20 21 22 23 24 25 26 27 28 29 30 31 32 33 34 35 36 37 38 39 40

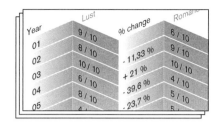

Year	Lust	% change	Romance
01	9 / 10		6 / 10
02	8 / 10	- 11,33 %	9 / 10
03	10 / 10	+ 21 %	10 / 10
04	6 / 10	- 39,6 %	4 / 10
05	8 / 10	- 23,7 %	5 / 10
	4 /		5 /

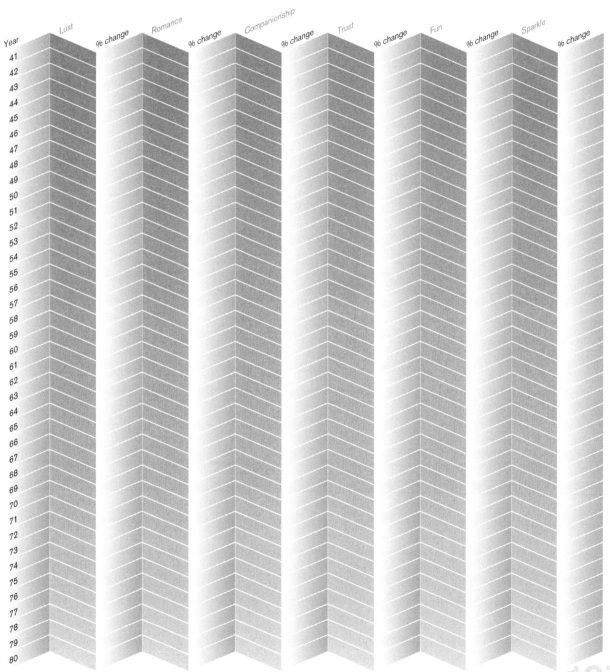

Year	Lust	% change	Romance	% change	Companionship	% change	Trust	% change	Fun	% change	Sparkle	% change
41												
42												
43												
44												
45												
46												
47												
48												
49												
50												
51												
52												
53												
54												
55												
56												
57												
58												
59												
60												
61												
62												
63												
64												
65												
66												
67												
68												
69												
70												
71												
72												
73												
74												
75												
76												
77												
78												
79												
80												

187

Trouble in Paradise

Even the most exemplary couple will occasionally feel like axe-murdering each other. This chapter is here to help channel those feelings into a mutually rewarding learning experience, and away from the criminal justice system.

Reminder for rough times

Fill this in on a good day, and keep at hand for less sunny moments. Refer to it before you decide to embark on any major row or legal proceedings. Careful! Do not tear up or spit on this page in anger. It hasn't done anything!

Why I love him...
....
....
....
....
....
....
....
....
....
....
....
....
....
Sealed with a kiss:..

Why I love her...
....
....
....
....
....
....
....
....
....
....
....
....
....
Sealed with a kiss:..

Our first row!

Subject:..

Who started it:..

Summary of her arguments:...

....

Summary of his arguments:..

....

Who won it: Her ☐ Him ☐ Both of you ☐ No one ☐

Did you have "angry sex" straight afterwards? Yes ☐ No ☐

Will it recur throughout your relationship? Yes ☐ No ☐ Very likely ☐

Our annoying habits

People don't divorce over great causes, they divorce over small tics. Even the most perfect human being has an irritating habit that drives their other half insane. Deal with yours here.

Her annoying habits

....	....	....
When she does this:............................	When she does this:............................	When she does this:............................
....	....	....
Supporting example:............................	Supporting example:............................	Supporting example:............................
....	....	....
Does she actually admit to it? Yes ☐ No ☐	Does she actually admit to it? Yes ☐ No ☐	Does she actually admit to it? Yes ☐ No ☐
Is it driving me to divorce? Yes ☐ No ☐	Is it driving me to divorce? Yes ☐ No ☐	Is it driving me to divorce? Yes ☐ No ☐
Is she making an effort to stop? Yes ☐ No ☐	Is she making an effort to stop? Yes ☐ No ☐	Is she making an effort to stop? Yes ☐ No ☐
....	....	....
When she does this:............................	When she does this:............................	When she does this:............................
....	....	....
Supporting example:............................	Supporting example:............................	Supporting example:............................
....	....	....
Does she actually admit to it? Yes ☐ No ☐	Does she actually admit to it? Yes ☐ No ☐	Does she actually admit to it? Yes ☐ No ☐
Is it driving me to divorce? Yes ☐ No ☐	Is it driving me to divorce? Yes ☐ No ☐	Is it driving me to divorce? Yes ☐ No ☐
Is she making an effort to stop? Yes ☐ No ☐	Is she making an effort to stop? Yes ☐ No ☐	Is she making an effort to stop? Yes ☐ No ☐

His annoying habits

....	....	....
When he does this:............................	When he does this:............................	When he does this:............................
....	....	....
Supporting example:............................	Supporting example:............................	Supporting example:............................
....	....	....
Does he actually admit to it? Yes ☐ No ☐	Does he actually admit to it? Yes ☐ No ☐	Does he actually admit to it? Yes ☐ No ☐
Is it driving me to divorce? Yes ☐ No ☐	Is it driving me to divorce? Yes ☐ No ☐	Is it driving me to divorce? Yes ☐ No ☐
Is he making an effort to stop? Yes ☐ No ☐	Is he making an effort to stop? Yes ☐ No ☐	Is he making an effort to stop? Yes ☐ No ☐
....	....	....
When he does this:............................	When he does this:............................	When he does this:............................
....	....	....
Supporting example:............................	Supporting example:............................	Supporting example:............................
....	....	....
Does he actually admit to it? Yes ☐ No ☐	Does he actually admit to it? Yes ☐ No ☐	Does he actually admit to it? Yes ☐ No ☐
Is it driving me to divorce? Yes ☐ No ☐	Is it driving me to divorce? Yes ☐ No ☐	Is it driving me to divorce? Yes ☐ No ☐
Is he making an effort to stop? Yes ☐ No ☐	Is he making an effort to stop? Yes ☐ No ☐	Is he making an effort to stop? Yes ☐ No ☐

Doghouse: If a problem isn't dealt with, this is where you end up. Beware!					
PROBLEM	Her	Him	Details	Time in doghouse	Repeat offence?
Annoying habit 1					
Annoying habit 2					
Annoying habit 3					
Annoying habit 4					
Annoying habit 5					
Annoying habit 6					
Lie					
White lie					
Damn lie					
Forgetting birthday					
Forgetting anniversary					
Forgetting to buy milk					
Not doing dishes					
Not taking out trash					
Not walking dog					
Not noticing new haircut					
Burning dinner					
Working late					
Coming home late					
Coming home drunk					
Not coming home					
Not listening					
Not calling					
Insulting relative					
Switching channels					
Not returning the video					
Not mowing lawn					
Not watering flowers					
Flirting with waiter					
Flirting with waitress					
Spilling wine on carpet					
Forgetting partner's name					

ENTER

Does he really love you? To find out for sure, go to a nearby field and pick 100 daisies. Pick their petals, and note the results. And remember: flowers don't lie.

He loves me:...................................../100 He loves me not:.................................../100

Does she really love you? To find out for sure, go to a nearby field and pick 100 daisies. Pick their petals, and note the results. And remember: flowers don't lie.

She loves me:................................./100 She loves me not:................................./100

Jealousy

The only third party allowed in your relationship should be your Couple's Book. Jealousy is only a sin if it's unfounded. If you suspect your partner of infidelity, investigate and challenge them within these pages.

Suspect	When	Where	Why	Suspect's rebuttal	Guilty
Her ☐ Him ☐					Yes ☐ No ☐ Probably ☐
Her ☐ Him ☐					Yes ☐ No ☐ Probably ☐
Her ☐ Him ☐					Yes ☐ No ☐ Probably ☐
Her ☐ Him ☐					Yes ☐ No ☐ Probably ☐
Her ☐ Him ☐					Yes ☐ No ☐ Probably ☐
Her ☐ Him ☐					Yes ☐ No ☐ Probably ☐
Her ☐ Him ☐					Yes ☐ No ☐ Probably ☐
Her ☐ Him ☐					Yes ☐ No ☐ Probably ☐
Her ☐ Him ☐					Yes ☐ No ☐ Probably ☐
Her ☐ Him ☐					Yes ☐ No ☐ Probably ☐
Her ☐ Him ☐					Yes ☐ No ☐ Probably ☐
Her ☐ Him ☐					Yes ☐ No ☐ Probably ☐
Her ☐ Him ☐					Yes ☐ No ☐ Probably ☐
Her ☐ Him ☐					Yes ☐ No ☐ Probably ☐
Her ☐ Him ☐					Yes ☐ No ☐ Probably ☐
Her ☐ Him ☐					Yes ☐ No ☐ Probably ☐
Her ☐ Him ☐					Yes ☐ No ☐ Probably ☐
Her ☐ Him ☐					Yes ☐ No ☐ Probably ☐
Her ☐ Him ☐					Yes ☐ No ☐ Probably ☐
Her ☐ Him ☐					Yes ☐ No ☐ Probably ☐

His Suspicions

She's working late	☐
She's buying new underwear	☐
She's stopped wearing her wedding ring	☐
She wants to try out new positions	☐
She has new tastes in music, film, art	☐
She spends more time on make-up	☐
Callers hang up inexplicably	☐
She hangs up inexplicably	☐
She spends more time on e-mail	☐
She has become lazy around the house	☐

Cheating score................................/10

Her Suspicions

He's working late	☐
He's buying new shirts/ties	☐
He's stopped wearing his wedding ring	☐
He wants to try out new positions	☐
He has tastes in music, film, art	☐
He spends more time on grooming	☐
Callers hang up inexplicably	☐
He hangs up inexplicably	☐
He spends more time on e-mail	☐
He's even lazier around the house	☐

Cheating score................................/10

Seven Year Itches Calculator

Start year of relationship: ....

+ 7 = ... + 7 = ...
+ 7 = ... + 7 = ...
+ 7 = ... + 7 = ...
+ 7 = ... + 7 = ...
+ 7 = ... + 7 = ...

Be extra suspicious of each other's behaviour in these notorious years!

Affairs

Who is allegedly having the affair? Her ☐ Him ☐

Have they confessed? Yes ☐ No ☐

If so, what excuse have they given?..

....

....

....

Identity of guilty party's partner in sin ("affairee")..........................

Affairee's version of events...

....

....

....

Did the offender claim their partner didn't understand them? Yes ☐ No ☐

Did the offender say they would leave their partner? Yes ☐ No ☐ Only after sex ☐

Was the offender visibly racked with guilt? Yes ☐ No ☐ Only after sex ☐

I, the affairee, swear that this is a true and faithful account of the affair.

Signature... Date..........................

Apology: Hey, I'm sorry about the whole thing ☐ I too feel wronged ☐

I intend to stalk you both until he/she is all mine! ☐ ❤

Affix evidence here
(photo/video/taped
phone call/ email/
credit card bill/phone
bill/underwear/other)

Is this evidence admissible in
a court of law? Yes ☐ No ☐

Contact details of
private investigator

....

....

....

....

Serial offenders

Affair 1	Forgiven ☐ I'm leaving you! ☐	Affair 26	Forgiven ☐ I'm leaving you! ☐
Affair 2	Forgiven ☐ I'm leaving you! ☐	Affair 27	Forgiven ☐ I'm leaving you! ☐
Affair 3	Forgiven ☐ I'm leaving you! ☐	Affair 28	Forgiven ☐ I'm leaving you! ☐
Affair 4	Forgiven ☐ I'm leaving you! ☐	Affair 29	Forgiven ☐ I'm leaving you! ☐
Affair 5	Forgiven ☐ I'm leaving you! ☐	Affair 30	Forgiven ☐ I'm leaving you! ☐
Affair 6	Forgiven ☐ I'm leaving you! ☐	Affair 31	Forgiven ☐ I'm leaving you! ☐
Affair 7	Forgiven ☐ I'm leaving you! ☐	Affair 32	Forgiven ☐ I'm leaving you! ☐
Affair 8	Forgiven ☐ I'm leaving you! ☐	Affair 33	Forgiven ☐ I'm leaving you! ☐
Affair 9	Forgiven ☐ I'm leaving you! ☐	Affair 34	Forgiven ☐ I'm leaving you! ☐
Affair 10	Forgiven ☐ I'm leaving you! ☐	Affair 35	Forgiven ☐ I'm leaving you! ☐
Affair 11	Forgiven ☐ I'm leaving you! ☐	Affair 36	Forgiven ☐ I'm leaving you! ☐
Affair 12	Forgiven ☐ I'm leaving you! ☐	Affair 37	Forgiven ☐ I'm leaving you! ☐
Affair 13	Forgiven ☐ I'm leaving you! ☐	Affair 38	Forgiven ☐ I'm leaving you! ☐
Affair 14	Forgiven ☐ I'm leaving you! ☐	Affair 39	Forgiven ☐ I'm leaving you! ☐
Affair 15	Forgiven ☐ I'm leaving you! ☐	Affair 40	Forgiven ☐ I'm leaving you! ☐
Affair 16	Forgiven ☐ I'm leaving you! ☐	Affair 41	Forgiven ☐ I'm leaving you! ☐
Affair 17	Forgiven ☐ I'm leaving you! ☐	Affair 42	Forgiven ☐ I'm leaving you! ☐
Affair 18	Forgiven ☐ I'm leaving you! ☐	Affair 43	Forgiven ☐ I'm leaving you! ☐
Affair 19	Forgiven ☐ I'm leaving you! ☐	Affair 44	Forgiven ☐ I'm leaving you! ☐
Affair 20	Forgiven ☐ I'm leaving you! ☐	Affair 45	Forgiven ☐ I'm leaving you! ☐
Affair 21	Forgiven ☐ I'm leaving you! ☐	Affair 46	Forgiven ☐ I'm leaving you! ☐
Affair 22	Forgiven ☐ I'm leaving you! ☐	Affair 47	Forgiven ☐ I'm leaving you! ☐
Affair 23	Forgiven ☐ I'm leaving you! ☐	Affair 48	Forgiven ☐ I'm leaving you! ☐
Affair 24	Forgiven ☐ I'm leaving you! ☐	Affair 49	Forgiven ☐ I'm leaving you! ☐
Affair 25	Forgiven ☐ I'm leaving you! ☐	Affair 50	Forgiven ☐ I'm leaving you! ☐

Top Tip! If you are having an affair, why not purchase a separate **THE Couple's BOOK**

I promise you I'm faithful! Her ☐ Him ☐

Words of wisdom 6

"In 1967, I was away for nurse training for two weeks," says Karen. "It was a cold winter. Søren was sick with urticaria, of a bad whelk. My sister Birgitte was helping him. When I was coming back, they were both crying to me. It happened. I was sad but it was better with my sister than a strange woman. But they repeated never in such a way. In the 1960 years, it was free love. Now I would be more strict. But it will not be a problem again soon, I do not regard."

197

Violent rows

If your rows are blistering, you may become too agitated to keep proper records. Worse still, you may damage the Couple's Book in the course of your quarrel. Hand it over to an impartial observer who will monitor the row and pick the winner from a safe distance.

Rational arguments	+3pts
Total points...	

Irrational arguments	+2pts
Total points...	

Circular arguments	+1pt
Total points...	

Insinuations	+4pts
Total points...	

Threats	−1pt
Total points...	

Insults	−2pts
Total points...	

Sarcastic remarks	+4pts
Total points...	

Sexual put-downs	+5pts
Total points...	

Door slammings	+1pt
Total points...	

Last word (+7 pts).. Delivered by..

Name...

Address...

....

Profession..

Link to the couple...

I, ...(her) agree that...(observer) is impartial, and I promise to accept their verdict on the row.

I, ...(him) agree that...(observer) is impartial, and I promise to accept their verdict on the row.

Date of row................................ Time of row............................... Duration of row................................ Row started by..

Rational arguments +3pts	Irrational arguments +2pts	Circular arguments +1pt
Total points........................	Total points........................	Total points........................
Insinuations +4pts	Threats −1pt	Insults −2pts
Total points........................	Total points........................	Total points........................
Sarcastic remarks +4pts	Sexual put-downs +5pts	Door slammings +1pt
Total points........................	Total points........................	Total points........................

Her:..........................pts Him:..........................pts Winner:.......................... Loser:..........................

Contingency plans

History is full of the cries of lovers wrenched from each other by accident, circumstance, or fate. Don't let the gods separate you forever: work out an action plan to meet up again whatever events may throw at your union.

Guide: if there's just the two of you left, refer to the Pillow Talk chapter for help in repopulating the Earth. If you have trouble breeding, positions 5, 13 and 56 are recommended.

Acts Of God: Prepare for the unthinkable.

In case: nuclear war breaks out and radioactivity is such that no one can surface for at least 10 years. Let's meet in the year 2018, near the remains of ....(nuked landmark) on...........................(date) at...........................(time).

In case: one of us gets lost in the shopping mall at a very busy time and the woman who pages people is off ill that day. Let's meet in aisle........................of the...supermarket, by the...brand of product.

In case: meteorite Zelda is about to strike and we are separated whilst evacuating planet Earth. Let's meet in.................................(year), during the...(solar eclipse), on refugee base..on the third ring of Saturn.

In case: one of us is kidnapped by terrorists by mistake and taken to a remote location. Let's meet by the information kiosk at local airport.., terminal...when the SWAT team bring you back.

In case: one of us has to work late and can't get the other on the phone. Let's meet at home/the pub just before last orders, near ....
....(local pub landmark).

In case: a nanotechnological experiment goes awry and grey goo takes over all living matter. Let's meet in..
....
....(to be confirmed).

Amnesia: Keep clues to jog each other's memory in case you get hit by a bus and can't remember ever being together.

Clues for her:

My name is...

My age is...

My partner is...

I've been with him since...

Our first kiss was...

He tastes of...

He smells of...

These things remind me of him...
....
....

These places remind me of him..

I love him because...
....
....

Clues for him:

My name is...

My age is...

My partner is...

I've been with her since...

Our first kiss was...

She tastes of...

She smells of...

These things remind me of her...
....
....

These places remind me of her..

I love her because...
....
....

If all else fails, buy a new Couple's Book and start your relationship afresh!

Arrested partner:

I swear I'm innocent! ☐
I did it, but I did it for us! ☐

Bereft partner:

I promise I will wait for you ....years ☐
I framed you to inherit your cash ☐

Choice of fruit for prison visits:

oranges ☐
bananas ☐

apples ☐

pears ☐

Cross out the days until she/he gets out. (ЦИ)

Escape plan (show through the glass when prison staff aren't looking):

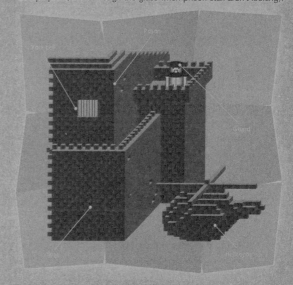

Poster

FREE..........................
.................(HER / HIS NAME)!

....
.................(HER / HIS NAME)
HAS BEEN WRONGFULLY
IMPRISONED! HELP FIGHT
THIS INIQUITOUS INJUSTICE
BY JOINING THE FREE

....
.................(HER / HIS NAME)
CAMPAIGN, DONATING
TO OUR CAUSE, AND
SIGNING OUR PETITION.

Petition

Petition to free..(him/her name)!

Signature........................
Signature........................
Signature........................
Signature........................
Signature........................
Signature........................
Signature........................
Signature........................
Signature........................
Signature........................
Signature........................
Signature........................
Signature........................
Signature........................
Signature........................
Signature........................
Signature........................
Signature........................
Signature........................
Signature........................
Signature........................
Signature........................
Signature........................
Signature........................
Signature........................
Signature........................

Saying sorry

Being in love means having to say sorry often and unprompted. When you are very close, you inevitably end up stepping on each other's toes. Tick one of these broken hearts every time you feel the need to apologize, explaining why below.

I'm sorry for:.................................
Apology accepted □ rejected □

I'm sorry for:.................................
Apology accepted □ rejected □

I'm sorry for:.................................
Apology accepted □ rejected □

I'm sorry for:.................................
Apology accepted □ rejected □

I'm sorry for:.................................
Apology accepted □ rejected □

I'm sorry for:.................................
Apology accepted □ rejected □

I'm sorry for:.................................
Apology accepted □ rejected □

I'm sorry for:.................................
Apology accepted □ rejected □

I'm sorry for:.................................
Apology accepted □ rejected □

I'm sorry for:.................................
Apology accepted □ rejected □

I'm sorry for:.................................
Apology accepted □ rejected □

I'm sorry for:.................................
Apology accepted □ rejected □

I'm sorry for:.................................
Apology accepted □ rejected □

I'm sorry for:.................................
Apology accepted □ rejected □

I'm sorry for:.................................
Apology accepted □ rejected □

I'm sorry for:.................................
Apology accepted □ rejected □

I'm sorry for:....................................
Apology accepted ☐ rejected ☐

I'm sorry for:....................................
Apology accepted ☐ rejected ☐

I'm sorry for:....................................
Apology accepted ☐ rejected ☐

I'm sorry for:....................................
Apology accepted ☐ rejected ☐

I'm sorry for:....................................
Apology accepted ☐ rejected ☐

I'm sorry for:....................................
Apology accepted ☐ rejected ☐

I'm sorry for:....................................
Apology accepted ☐ rejected ☐

I'm sorry for:....................................
Apology accepted ☐ rejected ☐

I'm sorry for:....................................
Apology accepted ☐ rejected ☐

I'm sorry for:....................................
Apology accepted ☐ rejected ☐

I'm sorry for:....................................
Apology accepted ☐ rejected ☐

I'm sorry for:....................................
Apology accepted ☐ rejected ☐

I'm sorry for:....................................
Apology accepted ☐ rejected ☐

I'm sorry for:....................................
Apology accepted ☐ rejected ☐

I'm sorry for:....................................
Apology accepted ☐ rejected ☐

I'm very sorry for:........................
Apology rejected ☐   rejected ☐

In case of trial separation

To come out of this one stronger, you will both need discipline. Take one of these detachable pages each and entrust the Couple's Book itself to a neutral friend or acquaintance until you get back together. Then follow the instructions.

Trial Separation Worksheet: Hers

ROW

Initiator of separation...

Reason for separation..

....

....

Subject of original row.............☐..........☐..................

....

....

Person to blame for original row..

....

Did the row get ugly? Yes ☐ No ☐

Words that can't be taken back...

....

....

....

....

SEPARATION

How long you agreed to separate for...

....

Why you loved him in the first place (reread every day)...........

....

Friends you will catch up with...

....

Honest opinion of friends about partner...................................

....

Record how much you miss him day by day:

COME BACK!

LONELY...

SULK SULK

MAD AT HIM

COWARD!

DAY 1 2 3 4 5 6 7 8 9 10 11 12 13 14 15 16 17 18 19 20

RECONCILIATION

Decision to patch things up: Yes ☐ No ☐

Decision to apologize: Yes ☐ No ☐

Conversation with his best friend to patch things up

....

....

....

....

His phone number..

No of minutes spent by phone before calling............................

His reaction...

....

....

....

....

Date of reconciliation..

Trial Separation Worksheet: His

ROW

Initiator of separation...

Reason for separation..
....
....
....

Subject of original row..
....
....
....

Person to blame for original row..
....

Did the row get ugly? Yes ❑ No ❑

Words that can't be taken back...
....
....
....
....

SEPARATION

How long you agreed to separate for...

Why you loved her in the first place (reread every day)...........
....
....

Friends you will catch up with..
....

Honest opinion of friends about partner......................................
....

Record how much you miss her day by day:

RECONCILIATION

Decision to patch things up: Yes ❑ No ❑

Decision to apologize: Yes ❑ No ❑

Conversation with her best friend to patch things up
....
....
....
....

Her phone number..

No of minutes spent by phone before calling.............................

Her reaction...
....
....
....

Date of reconciliation..

Letting go

This is make-or-break time. You are here because all else has failed. If the extreme measures below cannot save your relationship, then nothing can. Proceed (with great sadness) to the inevitable conclusion: the dissolution of your sacred bond.

Relationship DEF CON

This is your early warning system. Mark the change in your feelings for each other on this scale. As soon as either of you reaches zone 3, your relationship should immediately be put on full alert.

❶ I LOVE YOU!	❷ I LIKE YOU	❸ WHO ARE YOU?	❹ I PUT UP WITH YOU	❺ I HATE YOU!
Her ■ Him ■	Her ■ Him ■	Her ■ Him ■	Her ■ Him ■	Her ■ Him ■

Final ultimatums

DO.................... *stop seeing your secretary*

OR ELSE................ *I will decapitate her budgie*

YOU HAVE.............. *10 minutes*

DO..

OR ELSE..

YOU HAVE...

DO..

OR ELSE..

YOU HAVE...

DO..

OR ELSE..

YOU HAVE...

DO..

OR ELSE..

YOU HAVE...

DO..

OR ELSE..

YOU HAVE...

Emotional blackmailing techniques

a) You are so selfish, if you considered my feelings at all, you would
....

b) After all I've done for you,..
....is the least you can do for me.

c) Why are you ruining my life? All I ask is that you................................
....

d) Don't forget I know your deepest secret! I won't tell if..........................
....

e) If you don't..., we're through!

Mother to the rescue

His Mother talks to her: please don't break up with my boy, because
....
....

Her Mother talks to him: please don't ditch my daughter, for this reason
....
....

Did the two mothers' intervention help ☐ only make things worse ☐ ?

Last ditch attempt: *Benrik implore you to patch up your differences, if only for the sake of this Couple's Book!*

OK, we're sorry, what were we thinking, we're going to try real hard to make it work. ☐
No way! This book is largely responsible for the disintegration of our relationship! We're suing! ☐

Proceeding to next page? Yes ☐ No ☐

Dumper: Her ☐ Him ☐ Time:...Date:...

Place:...

Reasons (tick three maximum)   Reaction (tick three maximum)

I don't love you any more   ☐   Bastard/Bitch!   ☐

The spark has gone   ☐   This is a complete surprise   ☐

Our sex life sucks   ☐   I saw this coming   ☐

I can't stand your cooking   ☐   I've been miserable too   ☐

My sexual orientation has changed   ☐   I was about to dump you   ☐

I've found someone else   ☐   I didn't even realize we were together   ☐

Other (specify):...........................☐   Other (specify):...........................☐

How long did the relationship last?............years............months............days............hours

Mutual Decision. No one likes to be the one who's being dumped.
Here you may spare each other's feelings by ticking both boxes simultaneously.

I'm ending it ☐   ☐ I'm ending it too

Has closure been achieved? Her Yes ☐ No ☐ Why not?...

Has closure been achieved? Him Yes ☐ No ☐ Why not?...

Home truths Take this unique opportunity to let each other know what you really think.

Home truths about him:

1...

2...

3...

Home truths about her:

1...

2...

3...

Custody of the Couple's Book The dumped party gets custody of the Couple's Book, unless they were dumped for wronging the dumper in the first place and were thus ultimately responsible for the break-up ("passive dumping"). If both parties are equally to blame, open up the envelopes from "our first date" where you both had to guess how long the relationship would last. The closest guess gets custody. Visiting rights must include at least one evening a week, at least one weekend a month, and at least one week holiday a year. Both parties are responsible for the upkeep of the Couple's Book, and alimony must be paid by the dumper to that effect. Agreed alimony................per year. Disputes are to be referred to Benrik Limited, whose decisions are not subject to appeal.

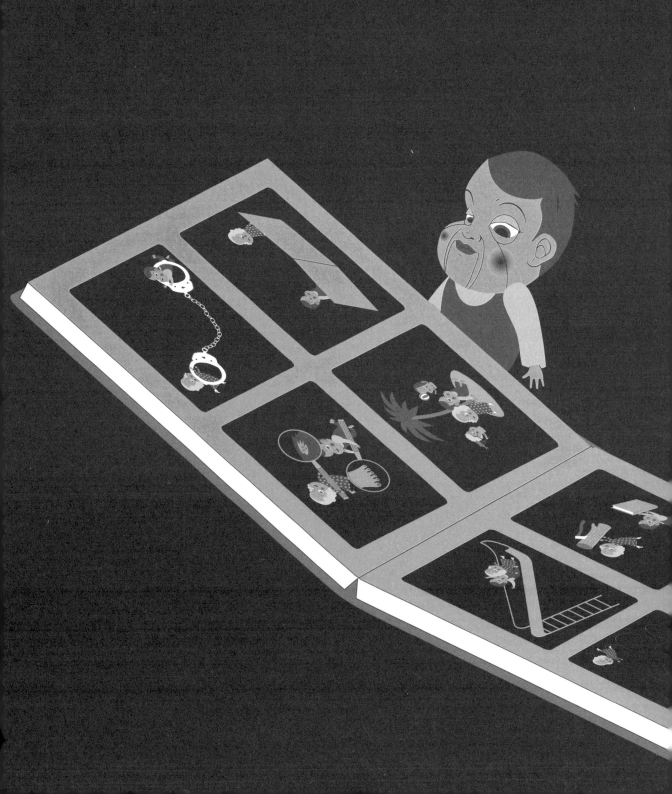

Ever After

It's never too early to plan your sunset years together, particularly in this day and age when both of you could end up pushing 100. Here you will find help with making grandchildren, ageing gracefully, and going down in history as one of the great couples of all time.

Happiest memories

The memories of your best moments together are your most precious possessions, that only time can steal. But don't wait for age to corrupt them: write down your happy memories as and when they occur.

Happy Memory 1

Date of memory:..
Details:.............*First kiss*.................................
Witnesses:..
Memory confirmed by her ☐ him ☐
Happiness rating:................................*10*......./10

Happy Memory 2

Date of memory:..
Details:...............*Wedding night*..........................
Witnesses:..
Memory confirmed by her ☐ him ☐
Happiness rating:..............................*10*........./10

Happy Memory 3

Date of memory:..
Details:...
Witnesses:..
Memory confirmed by her ☐ him ☐
Happiness rating:.../10

Happy Memory 4

Date of memory:..
Details:...
Witnesses:..
Memory confirmed by her ☐ him ☐
Happiness rating:.../10

Happy Memory 5

Date of memory:..
Details:...
Witnesses:..
Memory confirmed by her ☐ him ☐
Happiness rating:.../10

Happy Memory 6

Date of memory:..
Details:...
Witnesses:..
Memory confirmed by her ☐ him ☐
Happiness rating:.../10

Happy Memory 7

Date of memory:..
Details:...
Witnesses:..
Memory confirmed by her ☐ him ☐
Happiness rating:.../10

Happy Memory 8

Date of memory:..
Details:...
Witnesses:..
Memory confirmed by her ☐ him ☐
Happiness rating:.../10

Unhappy Memory 1

Date of memory:...

Details:...

Witnesses:..

Memory confirmed by her ☐ him ☐

Happiness rating:.../10

Unhappy Memory 2

Date of memory:...

Details:...

Witnesses:..

Memory confirmed by her ☐ him ☐

Happiness rating:.../10

Unhappy Memory 3

Date of memory:...

Details:...

Witnesses:..

Memory confirmed by her ☐ him ☐

Happiness rating:.../10

Unhappy Memory 4

Date of memory:...

Details:...

Witnesses:..

Memory confirmed by her ☐ him ☐

Happiness rating:.../10

Unhappy Memory 5

Date of memory:...

Details:...

Witnesses:..

Memory confirmed by her ☐ him ☐

Happiness rating:.../10

Unhappy Memory 6

Date of memory:...

Details:...

Witnesses:..

Memory confirmed by her ☐ him ☐

Happiness rating:.../10

Unhappy Memory 7

Date of memory:...

Details:...

Witnesses:..

Memory confirmed by her ☐ him ☐

Happiness rating:.../10

Unhappy Memory 8

Date of memory:...

Details:...

Witnesses:..

Memory confirmed by her ☐ him ☐

Happiness rating:.../10

Ageing gracefully

Using the Couple's Book on a regular basis ensures you have a higher than average chance of growing old together. Record the signs of ageing in each other, and rejoice in them as you would rejoice in the ageing of a fine Bordeaux.

She monitors his signs of ageing	37	38	39	40	41	42	43	44	45	46	47	48	49	50	51	52	53	54
Wrinkles																		
Sagging																		
Grey hairs																		
Age spots																		
Ear hair																		
Nose hair																		
Hair on pillow																		
Low tolerance for loud music																		
Low tolerance for young people																		
General crankiness																		
Country going to the dogs																		
Increasingly right-wing views																		
But I still find you attractive!																		

He monitors her signs of ageing	37	38	39	40	41	42	43	44	45	46	47	48	49	50	51	52	53	54
Wrinkles																		
Sagging																		
Grey hairs																		
Age spots																		
Hair on chin																		
Menopause																		
Low tolerance for loud music																		
Low tolerance for young people																		
General crankiness																		
Wearing of sensible shoes																		
Wearing of sensible underwear																		
Collecting supermarket coupons																		
But I still find you attractive!																		

"You're turning into your parent" alert

Dear, I'm afraid you're turning into your parents. Recently you said/did.. ....which is exactly what you've always said you hated in your mother/father.

Age at which you finally turn into your parents:

Her...

Him..

Keeping the Couple's Book young

Like you, your Couple's Book is subject to the vicissitudes of time. Act to safeguard it by reinforcing its binding with sellotape, as well as wrapping it in some protective material after nine to ten years' use.

57	58	59	60	61	62	63	64	65	66	67	68	69	70	71	72	73	74	75	76	77	78	79	80

57	58	59	60	61	62	63	64	65	66	67	68	69	70	71	72	73	74	75	76	77	78	79	80

Planning for grandchildren

You may well not yet have kids yourselves, but don't let that stop you from preparing the much more pleasurable experience of grandchildren. Picture yourself in the year 2037, surrounded by adoring bambinos, truly a 21st century Corleone.

Name..

Date of Birth...................................

Name..

Date of Birth...................................

Name..

Date of Birth...................................

Name..

Date of Birth...................................

Name..

Date of Birth...................................

Name..

Date of Birth...................................

Name..

Date of Birth...................................

Name..

Date of Birth...................................

Name..

Date of Birth...................................

Name..

Date of Birth...................................

Name..

Date of Birth...................................

Name..

Date of Birth...................................

What your grandchildren will call you	
HIM	Grandad ❑ Grandpa ❑ Grandfather ❑ Gramps ❑
HER	Grandma ❑ Granny ❑ Grandmother ❑ Nan ❑

Popular Year 2037 gifts for one's grandchildren. By 2037, kids will be able to sue their grandparents for psychological distress if they don't like their presents, so preorder now to avoid an expensive lawsuit and possible banishment to the muggy Centauris solar system. Gifts for natural grandchildren: a nice playstation 52, a bag of Krack Kokaine For Kidz!, or perhaps a cute little genetically-modified talking gerbil. Gifts for cloned grandchildren: another happy memory implant of you smiling over their cot.

Name......................................

Date of Birth...................................

Name......................................

Date of Birth...................................

Name......................................

Date of Birth...................................

Name......................................

Date of Birth...................................

Name......................................

Date of Birth...................................

Name......................................

Date of Birth...................................

Name......................................

Date of Birth...................................

Name......................................

Date of Birth...................................

Name......................................

Date of Birth...................................

Name......................................

Date of Birth...................................

Name......................................

Date of Birth...................................

Name......................................

Date of Birth...................................

Retirement

If you manage to stay together until retirement, you may as well stick it out. However without proper forward planning, you may end up united in poverty. Think ahead, and map out the climactic years of your coupling.

Couple's Will: Draw up your will together, with the help of this document.				
Potential heirs	Times they've visited lately	Other comments	Share of your fortune	Disinherited ✓
Child 1.........				☐
Child 2.........				☐
Child 3.........				☐
Child 4.........				☐
Distant relative 1.........				☐
Distant relative 2.........				☐
Pet 1.........				☐
Pet 2.........				☐
War buddy.........				☐
Kind stranger.........				☐
Signed: Her.........		......Him.........		

Topics of conversation You are going to have extended periods of free time together. Start making a shortlist of things to talk about now.

1..................
2..................
3..................
4..................
5..................
6..................
7..................
8..................
9..................
10..................
11..................
12..................
13..................
14..................
15..................
16..................
17..................
18..................
19..................
20..................

Words of wisdom 7

Søren and Karen are no longer young. "We are not young any longer," says Søren. "But she has not changed inward. Even if on the exterior she is covered with wrinkles and more bunions than my boat and blue veins such as cheese, and her hair has gone grey. Within, she is an angel." Karen blushes: "He may be balder and fatter but he still makes me smile, and that is the most important thing. The incontinence is not such a problem when you are used to it. If only he was not so groany!"

Put your names down for joint membership at an exclusive golf club now, and familiarize yourselves with this Couple's scorecard.

Golf club of choice:..

Waiting list:...years

His Name.............................. Her Name..............................

Course.................................. Date...................................

His Caddy.............................. Her Caddy..............................

His Handicap........................ Her Handicap........................

Hole	Yards	Par	His Score	Her Score
1				
2				
3				
4				
5				
6				
7				
8				
9				
Sub - Total				
10				
11				
12				
13				
14				
15				
16				
17				
18				
Sub - Total				
Total				

Plan your cruises

Cruise No 1
Ship..
Port of departure....................................
Ports of call...
Duration..
Captain's table   Yes ☐ No ☐

Cruise No 2
Ship..
Port of departure....................................
Ports of call...
Duration..
Captain's table   Yes ☐ No ☐

Cruise No 3
Ship..
Port of departure....................................
Ports of call...
Duration..
Captain's table   Yes ☐ No ☐

Cruise No 4
Ship..
Port of departure....................................
Ports of call...
Duration..
Captain's table   Yes ☐ No ☐

Cruise No 5
Ship..
Port of departure....................................
Ports of call...
Duration..
Captain's table   Yes ☐ No ☐

Cruise No 6
Ship..
Port of departure....................................
Ports of call...
Duration..
Captain's table   Yes ☐ No ☐

Cruise No 7
Ship..
Port of departure....................................
Ports of call...
Duration..
Captain's table   Yes ☐ No ☐

Cruise No 8
Ship..
Port of departure....................................
Ports of call...
Duration..
Captain's table   Yes ☐ No ☐

Cruise No 9
Ship..
Port of departure....................................
Ports of call...
Duration..
Captain's table   Yes ☐ No ☐

Cruise No 10
Ship..
Port of departure....................................
Ports of call...
Duration..
Captain's table   Yes ☐ No ☐

Ballroom dancing Learn these moves and you'll be "steps ahead" of the competition!

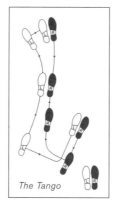

The Tango

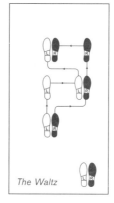

The Waltz

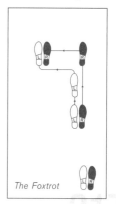

The Foxtrot

217

Looking back

As you look back over all these years, you must ask yourselves: was it worth it? Use our balance sheet to work out whether the happiness outweighed the inevitable sacrifices. Was the relationship a success?

Her Point
Of View

Opportunities I declined

1...
2...
3...
4...
5...

Worlds I might have conquered

1...
2...
3...
4...
5...

Potential lovers I scorned

1...
2...
3...
4...
5...

Lives I might have led

1...
2...
3...
4...
5...

Sacrifices I endured

1...
2...
3...
4...
5...

People I might have loved

1...
2...
3...
4...
5...

Places I might have explored

1...
2...
3...
4...
5...

Regrets I still harbour

1...
2...
3...
4...
5...

Adventures I might have had

1...
2...
3...
4...
5...

Was it worth it though?
Yes ☐ No ☐ Don't know ☐

His Point
Of View

Opportunities I declined	Worlds I might have conquered
1...	1...
2...	2...
3...	3...
4...	4...
5...	5...
Potential lovers I scorned	**Lives I might have led**
1...	1...
2...	2...
3...	3...
4...	4...
5...	5...
Sacrifices I endured	**People I might have loved**
1...	1...
2...	2...
3...	3...
4...	4...
5...	5...
Places I might have explored	**Regrets I still harbour**
1...	1...
2...	2...
3...	3...
4...	4...
5...	5...

Adventures I might have had

1...

2...

3...

4...

5...

Was it worth it though?
Yes ☐ No ☐ Don't know ☐

If both of you have ticked Yes, you may consider your relationship a success.

Till death do us part

You will eventually fade away into the night, but your love needn't. Ensure your joint flame burns bright forever with these surefire ways of immortalizing your love. And remember: your Couple's Book at least will survive you, and tell your glorious tale of love.

Sponsor a park bench in one of these prime locations

Central Park, New York $7,000
Luxembourg Gardens, Paris $5,000
Hyde Park, London $3,500
Güell Park, Barcelona $2,900
Villa Borghese, Rome $4,000
Ueno Park, Tokyo $19,000

This park bench was kindly bequeathed by ....
and.. By sitting on it, you honour their eternal love.

Funeral options

We wish to be buried together ☐
We wish to be cremated together ☐
We wish our ashes to be scattered together ☐
We wish our ashes to be kept in an urn together ☐

Compose your common epitaph here

....
....
....
....

What happens if one of you departs long before the other?

Dear survivor, (in case it's her), You were the love of my life Yes ☐ No ☐ Probably ☐

I wish you to remember me for my...

I give you the ok to fool around with someone else Yes ☐ No! ☐

Dear survivor, (in case it's him). You were the love of my life Yes ☐ No ☐ Probably ☐

I wish you to remember me for my...

I give you the ok to fool around with someone else Yes ☐ No! ☐

Dearly departed, I think of you hourly ☐
daily ☐ weekly ☐ often ☐ at Xmas ☐

By the
big cloud ■

At the angels'
concert ■

Just inside the
pearly gates ■

At the top of
the stairway ■

*Where shall we
meet in heaven?*

221

Benrik Limited
ARRANGED MARRIAGES

Benrik Limited's fans share the kind of sensibility that makes it difficult to find a suitable mate, or indeed any mate. This is why Benrik have decided to introduce a matchmaking facility for their followers! Simply fill in this questionnaire, send it c/o PFD Agency, 34 Russell St, London WC2B 5HA, UK, and Benrik will arrange your marriage with a Benrik fan of the opposing sex!*

Yes, I want Benrik Limited to arrange my marriage! ☐

Name.. Date of birth..

Address...

City... Postcode.. Country..

Telephone...(home) ....(work) ....(mobile)

Email...

I'm a big Benrik fan ☐ I own one/several books by Benrik ☐ I don't own any but I browsed one in a store once ☐

Gender (circle) M / F   Dates you are available for the wedding:.. Number of guests you would want to bring:....................

Would you wish to meet him/her before the wedding? Yes ☐ No ☐

Any other details/special requests? (e.g. do you require your spouse to speak fluent English?)..

....

....

I hereby agree to marry whoever Benrik deem to constitute a good match for me. Benrik do not require payment for performing this service, except for a one-off administration fee equivalent to 5% of the cost of the wedding. The choice of spouse is based entirely on the information provided.**

Date...Signature..

* Same sex marriages available in certain countries: request it under "Any other details?" ** You may also register online at www.couplesbook.com